# LOST
## AMUSEMENT PARKS
### OF NEW YORK CITY

# LOST
## AMUSEMENT PARKS
### OF NEW YORK CITY
### BEYOND CONEY ISLAND

Barbara & Wesley Gottlock

Published by The History Press
Charleston, SC 29403
www.historypress.net

Copyright © 2013 by Barbara H. Gottlock and Wesley Gottlock
All rights reserved

First published 2013

ISBN 978-1-5402-2481-1

Library of Congress CIP data applied for.

*Notice*: The information in this book is true and complete to the best of our knowledge. It is offered without guarantee on the part of the authors or The History Press. The authors and The History Press disclaim all liability in connection with the use of this book.

All rights reserved. No part of this book may be reproduced or transmitted in any form whatsoever without prior written permission from the publisher except in the case of brief quotations embodied in critical articles and reviews.

# CONTENTS

| | |
|---|---|
| Acknowledgements | 7 |
| Introduction | 9 |

**1. Manhattan**
| | |
|---|---|
| Fort George | 17 |

**2. Staten Island**
| | |
|---|---|
| South Beach | 33 |
| Midland Beach | 43 |

**3. Brooklyn**
| | |
|---|---|
| Golden City | 53 |

**4. Queens**
| | |
|---|---|
| North Beach | 71 |
| Rockaways' Playland | 85 |

**5. Bronx**
| | |
|---|---|
| Starlight Park | 91 |
| Clason Point | 106 |
| Freedomland | 113 |

| | |
|---|---|
| Index | 119 |
| About the Authors | 123 |

# ACKNOWLEDGEMENTS

While researching this project and our previous book about the lost amusement parks along New York's Hudson Valley, a whole new world opened up for us. Being relative novices to the genre, we were extremely fortunate to have been assisted by some of the country's foremost experts in amusement park–related niches. Many have spent decades researching the history of parks, roller coasters, Ferris wheels, carousels, vintage postcards and the like. Their willingness to share information and to set the facts straight was not only helpful but inspiring as well.

Three of these individuals deserve special kudos. Fred Dahlinger Jr. of Baraboo, Wisconsin, curator of circus history, Ringling Museum of Art in Sarasota, Florida, provided detailed documentation and images regarding carousels built long ago. Hopefully some of his research methodology has rubbed off on us. Similarly, Norman Anderson, professor emeritus at North Carolina State University, was kind enough to shed light on some of the Ferris wheels discussed in the following chapters. We spent time at the home of Bob Stonehill, whose collection of New York City postcards staggered us. Bob was a willing collaborator, and we cannot thank him enough for allowing us to use many of his cards in this book.

The staff at the Stephen A. Schwarzman Building of the New York Public Library's local history and map rooms was incredibly helpful and patient. Thanks to all of them.

We'd like to thank Gary Monti, director of Museum and Theater Operations at the Cradle of Aviation Museum/Nunley's Carousel on Long

## Acknowledgements

Island, for sharing some history and images of its historic carousel. The folks at the family-operated Clark's Trading Post (www.clarkstradingpost.com) were most helpful.

Once again, we wish to thank the Bronx County Historical Society, particularly librarian Laura Tosi. Also worthy of mention are the Staten Island Historical Society Library, Ira Kluger of the Canarsie Historical Society, Bill Cotter, Bill Brent, the Newburgh Free Library, Thomas Casey and the Friends of Starlight Park. Thanks to all of those who maintain websites related to amusement park history. If one has a need to research almost anything in New York State's rich history, you'll want to check www.fultonhistory.com sooner rather than later.

At The History Press, we would like to tip our hats to Whitney Landis and Jaime Muehl for their patience and for keeping us on track.

All images in this book, if not cited, are either in the authors' collection or in the public domain.

# INTRODUCTION

The history of amusement parks somewhat resembles one of their most popular attractions. Metaphorically, it's been a roller coaster ride. Not only have amusement parks transformed dramatically over the years, but also the ups and downs of the industry read almost like a good novel. It is worth looking back in time well before the blueprints for New York City's first parks were finalized.

Amusement parks are generally defined as the generic name for outdoor places of recreation to entertain large groups usually with a collection of rides and other attractions. Their roots can be traced back hundreds of years. Bakken, just north of Copenhagen, is generally regarded as the world's first amusement park when Kirsten Pill bought land that included natural springs in 1583. The healing power of the springs became the attraction, but soon thereafter various games and other forms of entertainment evolved. Magicians, jesters and jugglers performed. Simple games of chance, music and dancing became typical. Remarkably, Bakken still entertains large crowds each year well over four hundred years later.

By the seventeenth century, European pleasure gardens (or pleasure parks) made their debut. They provided a respite for the masses seeking relief from unpleasant living conditions in growing cities. While the beautifully landscaped gardens and fountains along walking paths were their focal points, other diversions were added to the menu. Beer gardens and food establishments developed. Lawn bowling, tennis and shuffleboard became staples.

New York City had its own pleasure park as early as 1767 with Vauxhall Gardens in lower Manhattan. It was loosely modeled after the historic

# Introduction

London park of the same name. Theater, music, gardens, fireworks and other forms of light entertainment filled the park. The term "pleasure park" held on for many years even after it made its way to America. One of the last usages of the term in New York was the Hudson Valley's Woodcliff Pleasure Park in Poughkeepsie (1927–41). It hosted the Blue Streak, the world's highest and fastest roller coaster at the time.

Another pleasure park, Jones's Wood, was located in Manhattan from the East River to what is now Third Avenue from Sixty-sixth to Seventy-fifth Streets. It consisted of nearly 150 wooded acres of entertainment. It grew over the years, starting in the first half of the nineteenth century. Its offerings included games of chance, fireworks, shooting galleries, races, animal rides, beer gardens, wrestling matches, picnic areas, food delights and horseback riding. Some of its land was parceled off as time went on, but a huge fire in May 1894 destroyed enough of the concessions, trees and structures (including the stables, where fifty horses perished) to render reconstruction financially prohibitive. Real estate values were climbing in the area, which no doubt hastened the decision to sell the property.

People started seeking more variety in the parks during the nineteenth century. Circus acts, balloon rides and crude "thrill" rides became more of a lure. It wasn't until the 1873 World's Fair in Vienna that the focus of the parks changed from mere relaxation to rides and attractions that offered more excitement. Fun houses, "pleasure wheels" (the precursor to the Ferris wheel), midways and rudimentary roller coasters made appearances.

But the World Columbian Exposition of 1893 (also known as the Chicago World's Fair) had an even greater impact on the evolution of amusement parks. In its six-month run, over twenty-seven million visitors (almost half the U.S. population at the time) were able to observe the latest advancements in amusements. "Modern" midways, new forms of concessions and ride innovations were introduced. The grand attraction was the debut of the Ferris wheel. The planners of the exposition put out a challenge to anyone who could create a unique attraction to outdo the Eiffel Tower, which was the star of the 1889 World's Fair in Paris.

George Ferris, a construction engineer from Illinois, designed a colossal "observational" wheel that became the centerpiece and the sensation of the fair. The mammoth wheel had a 264-foot diameter and spun its gondolas around on a forty-six-ton axle. Each of the thirty-six gondolas could hold up to 60 people. When filled, the ride held an astounding 2,160 people. Thereafter, Ferris wheels became fixtures at most amusement parks.

# Introduction

The fair spawned other amusement parks around the country, not the least of which was George Tilyou's Steeplechase Park in Coney Island in 1897. Coney Island began as a hotel and resort area in the mid-nineteenth century, with bathing, dining and dancing as the main attractions. When rail lines reached Coney Island in 1875, the beach area became available and affordable to the masses. The iconic Brooklyn amusement area saw a spurt of activity culminating with Frederic Thompson and Elmer "Skip" Dundy's purchase of Paul Boyton's Sea Lion Park. They opened the legendary Luna Park in 1903. The success of this venture encouraged entrepreneurs in all boroughs of New York City to build their own dream parks.

Two factors figured heavily in their strategic location plans. Most of the parks were built at trolley car stops or terminals to deliver the masses. These parks usually carried the generic name "trolley" park (also "electric park," referring to the trolley's power source). By 1911, well over half of all amusement parks in the country were owned by rail companies. The second consideration was water. To escape the summer's heat and oppressive conditions in Manhattan and the other boroughs, residents sought the refreshing water and breezes near beaches, bays and rivers. The builders were quick to respond.

In addition to Coney Island, the southern shores of Brooklyn and Queens were dotted with resorts, some of which evolved into amusement areas. The Rockaways, Brighton Beach, Bergen Beach and Manhattan Beach were among the successful resort areas. It wasn't long before each borough had at least one amusement or resort area of its own.

By the 1920s, amusement parks around the country and in New York City had reached what has been referred to as their "Golden Age." Despite Prohibition and World War I, the number of parks peaked at around 1,500 in 1919. But changes were on the way. The automobile, now accessible to growing numbers, afforded its owners the flexibility of driving to far-reaching places for respites without having to rely on rail lines to deliver them to specific locations. Trolley lines were being dismantled. Many parks closed as a result. The Great Depression of the 1930s dealt a serious blow to park owners. With most every dollar being spent on necessities, little was left for entertainment. Only about 400 parks remained in operation in the country by 1940. New York City fared no better. Coney Island and Rockaways' Playland struggled along. The other parks highlighted in this book were, with one or two exceptions, gone by 1950. Rising real estate values, fires and the construction of highways hastened their departures.

# Introduction

In the 1950s, amusement parks experienced a resurgence with the development of theme parks. The opening of Disneyland in Anaheim, California, in 1955 took theme parks to a whole new level. By the 1970s, corporations owned and operated many parks, leading to the "Coaster War"

# Introduction

This twilight photograph was taken from the top of the "chutes" at Coney Island's historic Dreamland. Note the sliver of beach area to the right. *Library of Congress.*

era. With new construction methods and technology, coasters and many other rides were designed for the non-squeamish. But by the new millennium, competition created a scenario where the number of park openings closely paralleled the number of closures.

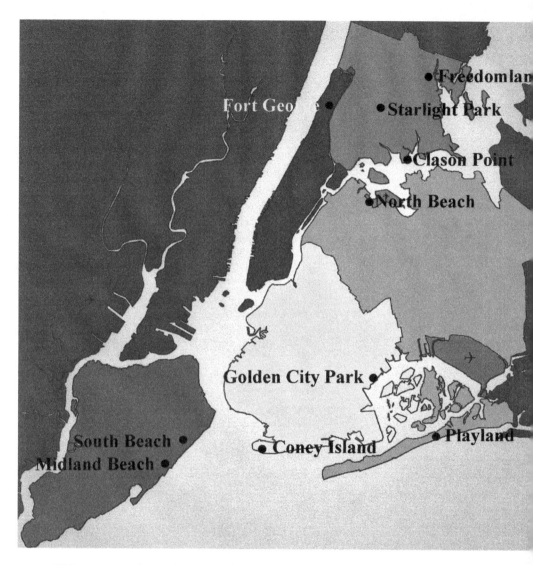

This map approximates the locations of the amusement parks discussed in this book. Note that many of the parks were located near bodies of water.

The following chapters highlight a number of amusement parks and areas in New York City that were created, at least in some part, to emulate Coney Island's success. While the story of Coney Island has been obsessively documented, very little is remembered about these smaller amusement parks and areas. They offered laughs, thrills and lasting memories each summer to millions of New York City residents.

Freedomland in the Bronx will get a shorter mention in this book than the others featured. Its inception came along quite a bit later (1960) than

## INTRODUCTION

the others, and there exists extensive information about its dramatic rise and fall (1964).

These parks hearken back to simpler times. Gone now are the men's bowler hats, suits and ties; the ladies' flowing dresses and bonnets; the strolling paths and gardens; the vaudeville shows, theatrical attractions and relatively tame rides. Despite these changes, there is a constant. There is something inside most of us craving relief from life's everyday routines. For many, it is still the amusement park.

# 1
# MANHATTAN

## FORT GEORGE

If one were to list all of Manhattan's varied assets, amusement parks would not be among them. But there was a time, before the island's real estate became so valuable, when a large amusement area flourished for many years.

The Fort George amusement area in the Washington Heights section of northern Manhattan was just a short boat ride away from the confluence of the Harlem and Hudson Rivers at Spuyten Duyvil Creek. The creek separates Manhattan and the Bronx. The amusement area is rarely mentioned along with the likes of Coney Island and Palisades Amusement Park. But at its peak, Fort George competed with both of those historic parks. It remains the largest open-air amusement park in Manhattan's history. Perhaps its abrupt demise in 1913, after only an eighteen-year run, denied the area its proper spot in the canon of the amusement industry giants.

The term "Fort George" refers to a strategic fortification constructed in northern Manhattan during the American Revolution. Revolutionary soldiers bravely engaged the British from the fort shortly after the Battle of Brooklyn in 1776, allowing General George Washington and his army an escape route to Westchester and New Jersey. Though Washington escaped successfully, the British continued their stronghold in New York City and eventually rebuilt Fort George. With the signing of the Treaty of Paris in 1783, the British abandoned the fort. It will be remembered as the last colonial position to fall on the island of Manhattan. Today, George Washington High School occupies the site.

# Lost Amusement Parks of New York City

In 1895, on land adjacent to the same hallowed grounds, a large and spectacular amusement area began to evolve. The location was ideal—perched atop cliffs along Amsterdam Avenue starting at 190th Street. Its western boundary was Audubon Avenue. The entertainment zone stretched north up to Fort George Avenue, where the Curve Music Hall was located, though most of the amusement rides were situated a few blocks south. At roughly one thousand feet above sea level, the vistas looking across the Harlem River were breathtaking. Some of the rides were designed to take advantage of the location's natural terrain to enhance thrills.

As with most other amusement parks of the era, trolley transportation was crucial. In the case of Fort George, the Third Avenue Railway System, which connected the Bronx to Manhattan, was the conduit. With a terminal near Fort George, the line delivered locals and residents from throughout the city to the park's doorstep for the sum of five cents from most Manhattan locations. The nearby Westinghouse Power and Electric Company provided the electricity for the park using alternating current. Eventually, Con Edison, which used direct current, would buy out Westinghouse.

Initially, the amusement area was an amalgam of hastily assembled structures to house sideshows, fortunetellers, smaller rides, shooting galleries, penny arcades and food concessions. The concessions were individually owned, largely by German businessmen. Many had been concessionaires on the Upper East Side's Jones's Wood, a popular working-class resort featuring beer gardens and many forms of entertainment. When that area was consumed by fire in 1894, many of the displaced entrepreneurs gravitated to the Fort George area along Amsterdam Avenue.

By 1899, a hotel and casino owned by John F. Schultheis was operating on the crest of the hill on Fort George Avenue. It eventually was heavily damaged by fire, the date of which remains unclear. The Great Handicap Race Track just north of Fort George Avenue opened before the turn of the century, as did the Harlem River Speedway. The speedway operated on what is now the Harlem River Drive from 155th Street to Dyckman Street. It featured harness races run by the well-heeled of Manhattan. It helped to attract more people to the nearby growing amusement area. It wasn't until 1919 that the roadway opened for motorists. In 1922, it was paved for the first time.

However, it wasn't until the arrival of the Schenck brothers, Joseph and Nicholas, that the amusement area achieved premier status. Joseph and Nicholas Schenck became, by far, the amusement area's major players. The Schencks emigrated from Russia in 1893, when Nicholas was eleven years

The Old Barrel was perched on a cliff along Amsterdam Avenue at Fort George. Its proprietors, the Schenck brothers, went on to build Paradise Park. Note the coaster to the right. *Courtesy of Jason Minter.*

old and Joseph was two years older. As very young men, their business acumen grew, yielding several successful small businesses. Joseph bought and operated a pharmacy where he had worked as a lad. While visiting the bustling amusement area one weekend during 1904, the brothers quickly realized that there was money to made at Fort George. They quickly established a modest-sized (fifteen- by twenty-five-foot) drinking establishment called the Old Barrel. They were rewarded with success in more ways than they probably ever imagined.

They soon befriended a customer at the Old Barrel by the name of Marcus Loew. Loew had already achieved some fame and fortune as an owner of penny arcades, nickelodeons and theaters in New Jersey and New York, including the Royal Theater in Brooklyn. The trio built a vaudeville stage adjacent to the Old Barrel in 1905 that garnered even more profit. A cane board and knife board were added in the second season. Loew, also seeing the potential at Fort George, agreed to lend Nicholas and Joseph the funds necessary to construct a separate entertainment complex to be named Paradise Park at the Fort George amusement area in 1905.

The Fort George Amusement Company was organized on February 8, 1905, listing Joseph Schenck as president, Marcus Loew as vice-president, Nicholas Schenck as treasurer and William Mundt as secretary. Initial capital assets were listed as $40,000. These events, along with the contributions of scores of other entrepreneurs, would lead to the amusement area being dubbed "Manhattan's Coney Island."

The thrilling rides and other recreational diversions at Paradise Park became wildly popular and spurred even more growth. Only a power failure on August 9, 1905, marred the first season. The entire park went dark. Passengers in the top cars of the giant Ferris wheel panicked in the darkness on the crowded weekend night. Their screams could be heard throughout the park. Some threatened to jump and had to be restrained by fellow riders. People inside the Old Mill had no means of escape in the dark tunnels. Its boats remained still as water ceased to flow inside the ride. Fortunately, a gunboat and several yachts in the river, realizing the emergency, shone their search lights on the park, alleviating further panic. Power was eventually restored, and there were no casualties.

Around the time Paradise Park was gaining a foothold at Fort George, two hugely successful figures in the amusement industry, Elmer "Skip" Dundy and Frederic Thompson, made a splash with some startling news. Thompson and Dundy were best known for developing and building the sensational Luna Park at Coney Island and the Hippodrome in Manhattan. On March 31, 1906, they announced to the press that they would be building, in their words, an "immense amusement empire unlike anything in existence" and an "uptown wonderland" at Fort George. It would be called Vanity Fair.

Based on the seventeenth-century classic *Pilgrim's Progress* by John Bunyan, the theme park, as they envisioned it, would be an architectural and amusement colossus with typical marketplaces of that era. The centerpiece would have been an extravagant show featuring decoratively dressed chorus girls, majestic fountains and "modern" lighting effects. They even went so far as to take out a twenty-five-year lease on the Jennings Estate, the equivalent of one hundred city lots. Plans were drawn up to construct an electric railway from the foot of the Dyckman Street station that eventually would wend its way up to Audubon Avenue.

But Skip Dundy died suddenly on February 5, 1907, ending a most colorful life and probably putting the Vanity Fair project to an end. But that did not deter Frederic Thompson from moving forward with other plans at Fort George. He made an announcement to the press on March 26, 1907. Thompson detailed plans for the construction of an airship terminal at Fort George. Airships ninety feet in length would dock at Fort George atop a one-hundred-foot-high platform. Passengers would ascend in an elevator to the loading platform. The ships would float to a terminal atop a building at

At least two entrances admitted patrons (for a ten-cent fee) to Paradise Park. Posted bills next to this ornate portal advertised the park's roller-skating rink. *Courtesy of Bob Stonehill.*

Broadway and Twenty-ninth Street. From there, the journey would continue to Coney Island, where the passengers would be met by a band atop the "Trip to the Moon" attraction, which he owned. Thompson could cash in on both ends of the airship's journey. It was never built.

But Thompson still was not finished at Fort George. A small park under both Thompson's and Dundy's names opened at Fort George in June 1907. The feature attraction was Bostock's "Rounders," considered to be one of the most elaborate carousels in the world. It is not known if the planned figure-eight toboggan, miniature railroad and circle swing were all in operation in that year.

The pair had made fortunes but had spent a lion's share of it on yachts, enormous restaurant tabs, drinking, other indulgences and extravagances. Skip Dundy's passing left Thompson awash in a sea of lofty ambitions and complicated finances. It is possible that Thompson just gave up on Fort George as finances became more pressing and he missed his partner's relative stability. Thompson never paid rent on the Fort George property and was in arrears to the tune of $150,000 when a list of his creditors was drawn up. Besides, Fort George was beginning to look like a risky investment at this juncture considering its limited space for expansion. His drinking problems worsened, and he eventually lost Luna Park to creditors. Although he subsequently attempted several smaller ventures, he filed for bankruptcy in 1912. He died in 1919. Friends had to take up a collection to purchase a headstone.

But with Paradise Park on its enclosed three-acre site in full swing starting in 1905, the Fort George amusement area had something to please almost every taste judging by the crowds it drew. Up to 100,000 visitors per day, according to a 1907 newspaper account, arrived by trolley or horse and buggy. Local residents merely walked to the midway. Its features included two highly visible Ferris wheels, tunnel boat rides, skating rinks, a toboggan coaster that slithered down the cliff toward the Harlem River, swimming pools and two other world-class roller coasters to please enthusiasts of that genre. Three beautiful carousels entertained young and old. Two of the carousels were built expressly for Fort George by the renowned Philadelphia Toboggan Company. One was commissioned in 1905 and the other in 1908. In addition, countless midway concessions lined Amsterdam Avenue.

One coaster built in 1907 was aptly nicknamed the "Rough Rider." It replaced a tamer coaster that had operated since the opening of Paradise Park. The original coaster was not bereft of problems. During its construction, a worker was killed and several more were seriously injured when some pilings

# Manhattan

The Rough Rider coaster brought thrills to many both at Paradise Park and later at the Schenck Brothers Palisade Park. *Courtesy of Bob Stonehill.*

collapsed on March 28, 1905. The Rough Rider's run was checkered as well. The third-rail coaster required a motorman to operate it. In essence, it was akin to a subway ride in open-air cars hurtling down the side of the hill with figure eights and hairpin turns to make it more "interesting." Electric motors hauled the cars back up the hill after their run. It is doubtful even its legendary builder, William F. Mangels of Coney Island fame, realized the thrills he created for the price of ten cents. The ride lasted two and a half minutes on a track seventh-eighths of a mile long. Its maximum height was seventy-five feet.

According to reports, some motormen had a diabolical streak. Instead of coasting or slowing down over or around certain curves and hills as they were instructed to do, some pushed forward on the lever. Riders often got the thrill of their lives. Unfortunately, some were injured as they were thrown from the cars. Lawsuits abounded. After the first fire to strike Fort George Amusement Park in 1911, the Rough Rider was dismantled and reopened as a new attraction at the Schenck Brothers Palisade Park. Interestingly, the ride ran in reverse of its operation at Fort George. The ride began at the base of the cliff until it reached the top, and then the thrills began.

Mangels also designed the "Tickler" at Fort George, a tame ride by comparison. The ride, introduced by Mangels at Coney Island, was "designed to jostle, jolt, and jounce its riders about in their seats when the ride was in motion," according to its originator. The bumping and whirling of the cars down an incline careening off rubber obstacles like a pinball machine created a fair amount of body contact. This action led to it being called "the perfect date ride for couples."

Vaudeville shows and dancing were popular at Fort George. At least four music halls—the Trocadero at 190th Street, the Star at 192nd Street (near the rear entrance to Paradise Park), the Paradise Park Music Hall and, at the northern reaches of the entertainment zone, the Curve at 197th Street—offered quality vaudeville and musical acts. The Trocadero's acts were provided by agents Sam and Freeman Bernstein. The Star was operated by C.J. Johne, and its six-piece orchestra was a popular draw. There was no admission charge for the Paradise Park Music Hall. Profits were generated through the sale of food and refreshments. Featured regular performers at Fort George included the popular Professor Ziegler and his German band.

The midway was no less entertaining with its nine saloons, five shooting galleries and the omnipresent freak sideshows. Among the sideshow attractions were the "Human Ostrich" and "Ramses the Giant Killer of the Zambesi." The former amazed patrons by swallowing items ranging from a pack of tacks to curled rancid sandwiches left out on the park's picnic

This Tickler ride and the Rough Rider at Fort George were designed by William Mangels (1866–1958), a major player in the development of amusement parks around the turn of the twentieth century. *Courtesy of Bob Stonehill.*

tables. Ramses, a huge man who displayed feats of strength, was said to have escaped unaided from a horde of Italian soldiers. Children were able to enjoy the pony track, the roller rink or the open-air swimming pool. When their parents wished to be alone for a spell, a facility was available for supervision of the tots (for a fee).

Restaurants and other food concessions were kept busy by the influx of visitors, particularly on the weekends. One popcorn and candy (taffy was a specialty) concession at Fort George was owned and operated by Mary Gish, mother of legendary movie queen Lillian Gish. Lillian's father had left the family before she could even form memories of him. Mary Gish went about saving what little money she could from a small business in Brooklyn and some sporadic acting work in order to purchase the space at the park in the summer of 1905. According to her memoirs, Lillian's job at the age of eleven or twelve was to stand on a box and repeat over and over in as plaintive a voice as possible, "Would you like to buy some candy?"

Lillian also reminisced about the day her younger sister, Dorothy, went missing among the hubbub at Fort George. Frantically, the family searched among all the stands and stalls until they spotted her standing high on the snake charmer's platform during a performance. Pushing through the crowd, Mary nearly fainted when she saw a huge snake wrapped around her daughter's body. Little Dorothy was smiling and appeared oblivious to the snake. She was duly punished.

When business at the candy stand was slow, the girls exercised the ponies at Mr. Craemer's pony concession. They rode them bareback and fast. One day, little Dorothy fell off her pony. She was rushed to the hospital, where she was treated for a compound fracture of her arm. Meanwhile, Lillian, left behind at the park, feared the worst had befallen her sister. It was evening before Mary returned from the hospital with Dorothy, but no one could find Lillian. Concerned workers at Fort George had been scouring the area for the better part of the day. Finally, Mary discovered the terrified Lillian crouching in the machinery shed at the center of a carousel. She quickly reassured her daughter that everything was going to be all right. Lillian claimed that her early horseback riding at Fort George spurred a love of that skill that endured throughout her storied life.

But after two years, the Gish concession burned to the ground, leaving the family with little income. Reluctantly, Mary returned to acting and strongly encouraged her young daughter to do so as well. The rest is history.

The Fort Wendel Hotel and Café (also known as the Fort Wendel Hotel and Amusement Center) was a popular resort and ride area at Fort George.

Its all-ladies' orchestra was highly acclaimed. The building was built just off Amsterdam Avenue at around 194th Street and extended down the cliff. The builder and proprietor, Captain Louis Wendel, was a colorful figure. Wendel commanded the National Guard's First Battery Armory on West 66th Street. Wendel became a wealthy man but certainly not on his military income alone. In December 1906, Wendel was indicted on a litany of charges. Among them were taking kickbacks in return for jobs at the armory, renting the armory's horse stalls to private citizens, operating an illegal bar on the premises and padding expense accounts. He was also charged with using government workers to perform labor at his Fort George complex. Wendel was discharged by court-martial in April 1907. The Fort Wendel Hotel and Café mysteriously burned shortly thereafter. He died in 1914.

A large rink hosted roller skaters in the summer and, it is believed, ice skaters in the winter. It debuted in time for the opening of the 1907 season. In June 1907, a most unusual wedding was held at the rink. Raymond Barrett and his nineteen-year-old fiancée, Susan Pierce, first met at Fort George. In celebration of that event, they, along with the minister, laced on roller skates for the ceremony that took place on the rink's floor. Rings exchanged, the newlyweds were joined on the floor by five hundred couples. They all skated to "Love Me and the World Is Mine." They honeymooned in Atlantic City.

Improvements to the area were made in 1906 and 1907 to ensure that patronage would grow. A *Variety* article indicated that a "sprucing up" was needed. This perhaps spurred many of the changes. Another Ferris wheel, topping out at seventy feet and with sixteen passenger cars, appeared on the scene in 1906. A thirty-foot-high slide at Paradise Park was added late in the year. Speed and Darcy's "Old Mill" was refurbished with new effects inside its darkened cavern. Several of the dance halls expanded. More lights illuminated the area, much to the chagrin of nearby residents. An elevator installed by the Reno Inclined Elevator Company was already in place. No longer would patrons be required to scale the steep steps from Amsterdam Avenue up the hill to Audubon Avenue. Fresh coats of paint were applied. In addition, a parking garage was added for those fortunate enough to own vehicles. The crowds continued to come.

Petty crimes had plagued the area for several years. Things were brought under control when the 152nd Precinct, under the direction of newly assigned Sergeant Patrick Corcoran, instituted changes in patrols along peripheral areas and cracked down on swindling concessionaires. To appease local residents, the area was closed by 11:00 p.m. every evening starting in September 1908.

# Manhattan

The Fort George amusement area as seen from the Bronx across the Harlem River.

In June 1908, plans were filed by Frederic Thompson for a "Roli Rider," a circle wheeler with a thirty-two-foot-diameter platform built of wood and steel at a cost of $3,000. It would accommodate sixty-six riders at a time, and they would be spun around six times per minute. Thompson planned to lease the ride for the season. Since no images of the ride exist, it is unclear if it came to fruition, especially considering Thompson's troubles.

The clientele at the Fort George amusement area was generally considered more working class than Coney Island's attendees. But nonetheless, respectable behavior was expected. Arguably the area's finest establishment, the Fort George Hotel and Casino catered to a wealthier clientele, many of whom enjoyed its offerings of gambling, dancing, drink and fine food. But as Fort George entered the second decade of the century, the character of the area began to change.

Women, whether alone or in groups, had always felt secure at Fort George. Suddenly, many reports of harassment—and worse—surfaced. People were no longer dressing in their Sunday finest. Local residents became increasingly concerned about noise, rowdiness and public intoxication. Petty crimes were mounting again. In the fall of 1909, even the local police precinct located on 152$^{nd}$ Street suggested to city officials that the park should be shuttered.

Even citizens from the Morris Heights section of the Bronx across the river were calling for changes. They were tiring of the late-night cacophony emanating from the rides and the fireworks. One of their civic groups enlisted the help of a representative, George Budlong, to intervene. Budlong met with Joseph Schenck. He told Schenck he'd tell his constituency everything would be worked out in exchange for a seventy-five-dollar payment. When Budlong returned to pick up his compensation, Schenck introduced him to two of his "aides," who were really newspaper reporters. Once the bribe changed hands, authorities were called, and Budlong was arrested. He was later convicted.

While the Schenck brothers maintained ownership in Paradise Park at Fort George, they formed another company, the Palisades Realty and Amusement Company, in February 1910. They purchased the Palisades Amusement Park in Cliffside Park, New Jersey (rechristened the Schenck Brothers Palisade Park). The Schencks used some of the proceeds from the sale of their vaudeville stage operation at Fort George to finance the purchase. They revitalized the New Jersey amusement park with the construction of some of the largest rides in the area and the nation's largest saltwater wave pool. Also, by 1910, Nicholas Schenck alone was listed in city records as a board officer on no fewer than a dozen corporations, including his vice-presidency of the Fort George Amusement Company. But Fort George no longer seemed to be the priority of Joseph and Nicholas Schenck.

Also around this time, real estate speculators were eyeing the area for housing development. They felt that the amusement area was an obstacle to their interests. Local residents lobbied for the construction of a public park, but the speculators fought that notion, realizing the possibility of huge profits as real estate values soared in Manhattan. The city rejected the idea of a park, stating that it was not in a strong enough financial position to lose the tax revenue that the amusement park generated. The city's response was supported with figures, including the fact that many schools were already facing class sizes of up to sixty children in that very neighborhood. In any event, some construction of new buildings began along the perimeter of the amusement area.

Calling it an "immoral" resort at a meeting on February 26, 1910, members of the Washington Heights Taxpayers Association, acting on behalf of several civic groups, once again petitioned that the amusement area be razed. It was no surprise that developers fully backed the group. Like the citizens of Morris Heights, the nearby residents protested the squeals and groans of the Ferris wheels, the repeating melodies of carousel music, the "hilarity" of the dance halls, fireworks and the bright lights burning late on the weekends. Sleepless nights were at the crux of their issues.

On December 10, 1911, an arsonist attempted to burn down the park. The suspect was quickly spotted by a local resident, who took chase but was unable to collar the culprit under the cloak of darkness. His exact motive will never be known. The wind-blown flames destroyed the Star Music Hall (formerly the historic Star Hotel, dating back to colonial times), the Fort George Hotel, Paradise Park's dance hall, a popular tavern and some smaller concessions. The three-alarm blaze also threatened the nearby Isabella Geriatric Home. Despite the setback, the 1912 season opened as scheduled.

But the park's fatal blow came on June 9, 1913. Another suspicious fire, described by many fire officials as the most "spectacular" they had ever seen, nearly destroyed the entire amusement park in the early morning hours. The Paradise Park night watchman, Dominick Barnot, quickly reported that several buildings were ablaze, but it was too late. Within ten minutes, another dance hall outside of Paradise Park was fully engulfed in flames that were already soaring more than one hundred feet into the air. The conflagration was eventually observed as far south as Forty-second Street. Citizens across the river in the Morris Heights section of the Bronx spilled out of their homes to view the spectacle. Spared were only some of the smaller amusement areas, a few food concessions, the pool, one carousel and a billiards parlor.

Firefighters, realizing that they could not stave off the inferno at the park, allowed the park's grand structures to burn. They turned their attention to nearby residential and business buildings instead. Thousands descended on the Fort George area, despite the early hour, to view the inferno. Nearby tenants formed bucket brigades to toss water on their roofs to prevent the sparks from igniting their buildings.

The amusement structures were fully engulfed in flames within thirty minutes. First to collapse were the roller coasters, followed by the giant Ferris wheels, the carousels and the skating rink. At one hundred feet high, the largest Ferris wheel succumbed early, and the flames were seen for miles around until it collapsed. Nearly all of the structures at Paradise Park were destroyed or severely damaged. On the day after the fire, thousands roamed the park's acreage to observe the changed landscape and smoldering remains and to scavenge for mementos. Only a carousel (Philadelphia Toboggan Company #15) remained relatively unscathed.

Barely had the last embers extinguished when Joseph Schenck announced to the press on June 14 that he would rebuild Paradise Park. It would not only be grander, but he also proposed building a giant roof over a good portion of the park so visitors could come and enjoy the amusements rain or shine. He would have it ready by the following season. Community protests against rebuilding grew and led to news headlines such as "Citizens Fight New (Amusement) Park" in the *New York Sun* on September 25, 1913.

The concept of a public park was brought up again, but the city maintained its stance that tax revenue could not be sacrificed.

The Schencks' lease on Paradise Park was due to expire around this time. It is doubtful anyone will ever know if they had truly planned to stay on. Some reports suggest that the brothers transported salvaged remnants from Fort George to the Schenck Brothers Palisade Park. Nobody else came forth with any plans to resurrect the park. Some smaller businesses probably struggled on into 1914. A movement by local concerned citizens' groups finally led to the cancellation of all licenses and leases at the Fort George amusement area. The cleanup of the area was "brought about with no small difficulty," according to a *New York Times* account. The amusement area's land stayed in limbo for a number of years. Eventually, parcels of land were sold. The owner of Thom's Scenic Railway, one of the longer holdouts, sold his 100- by 228-foot parcel, all equipment included, at public auction for $25,000 on January 27, 1916.

The Schenck brothers retained some property at Amsterdam Avenue and 193rd Street. In August 1917, they floated the idea of building two large movie studios under their still viable Fort George Amusement Company, of which Marcus Loew remained a partner. A newspaper account on December 29 again reiterated their desire. The project never got off the ground.

By around 1919, the brothers had begun to lose interest in the day-to-day operations of their Schenck Brothers Palisade Park in New Jersey. They turned their focus instead to the growing film industry in Hollywood. They eventually sold their interest in the Schenck Brothers Palisade Park in 1935 to the Rosenthal brothers, who had enjoyed a modicum of success at Coney Island. By that time, the Schencks and Loew were firmly entrenched in Hollywood. They went on to make fortunes in California. Joseph Schenck became board chairman of United Artists. He later founded 20th Century Fox along with Darryl Zanuck. Loew's Incorporated became a hugely successful chain of movie theaters. Nicholas Schenck was Loew's Incorporated's president and general manager and later became the head of Metro-Goldwyn-Mayer.

Interestingly, a newspaper account on July 26, 1919, indicated that some of the amusement area's unsold acreage was being used as a public vegetable garden. Approximately 150 separate garden plots were tended by volunteers. On a somber note, it was reported that some of the bean and squash plants' vines grew on a trellis that was the remains of one of the amusement area's carousel houses.

With the amusement area now just a memory, local groups lobbied for a new high school to be built on the spot of historic Fort George. Despite

The Fort George Garden was a drinking and eating establishment on Fort George Avenue.

much debate and competition from other interested areas of Manhattan, they prevailed. The new George Washington High School became a reality in 1925. Its distinguished alumni include news reporter Edwin Newman, opera singer Maria Callas, former secretary of state Henry Kissinger, famed economist Alan Greenspan, singer Harry Belafonte and athletes Rod Carew and Manny Ramirez.

In 1928, the City of New York purchased the remaining tracts of the former amusement area's grounds east of Amsterdam Avenue. The city eventually extended Highbridge Park northward to fill the void. Today's park is starkly tranquil compared to the fervor and excitement on the grounds around a century ago. Remarkably, no historic signs or plaques mark the spot where the amusement area once brought enjoyment to so many.

On a more positive note, the amusement area's only carousel (PTC #15) to survive the great fire of 1913 has been preserved. Until 2009, it was the centerpiece attraction at the Palisades Center shopping mall in West Nyack, New York, where it operated for eleven years. An organ that played for one of the carousels has been lovingly preserved and now resides in England. These are the only treasures known today to exist from the Fort George era.

# 2
# STATEN ISLAND

## South Beach

Giovanni da Verrazano, an Italian explorer sailing under French sponsorship, was the first European to pass Staten Island in 1534 when he sailed through the narrows to New York Bay. In 1609, Henry Hudson, an English explorer sailing under the Dutch flag, sailed up the present-day Hudson River in his ship the *Halve Maen* (*Half Moon*) and named the island *Staaten Eyelandt* after the Dutch Parliament.

It was not until 1661, after an agreement was reached between the Native Americans and the Europeans, that the Dutch were finally able to establish the first permanent settlement in Staten Island. The settlement, which was called *Oude Dorp* (Old Town), was near the present-day South Beach. South Beach is located on the southeastern shore of Staten Island about four miles from Saint George.

South Beach, as many other resort areas in New York City, emerged as transportation became more readily available. In July 1884, the Staten Island Rail Transit began rail service from Tompkinsville to Tottenville, Staten Island. Later that year, the service was extended to Saint George. It was this rail service that opened up Staten Island to thousands of New Yorkers looking for ways to escape the teeming tenement life of Manhattan and Brooklyn. They began flocking to Staten Island's seashore to enjoy the beaches and fresh breezes the bay provided.

Happyland had a lagoon at its center. Professor Karas' European Novelties stand was one of the many concessions at the park. *Courtesy of Bob Stonehill.*

*Opposite:* Tirelli's Whip was one of the earliest rides at Happyland. *Courtesy of Fred Dahlinger Jr.*

The shore at South Beach became so popular that on July 10, 1892, the *Press*, a New York newspaper started in 1887, offered a free "Sail Down the Bay" to South Beach. A barge took passengers past the Statue of Liberty, Castle Williams on Governor's Island, Robbins' Reef lighthouse, Fort Wadsworth, Staten Island and Fort Hamilton, Brooklyn, to the wharf at South Beach. Once there, the picnickers found "plenty of entertainment for everyone."

At that time, the beach was the main attraction, but other entertainment was also available. There was a carousel and Noah's Ark, where children rode around and around on the animals accompanied by music. In addition, there were groves, swings and plenty of room to play myriad games. Numerous hotels lined the beach. If a person did not wish to venture onto the sand, he or she could sit on a covered veranda, enjoy the cool breeze and take in the activity all around. Most of the hotels provided tables for basket parties, as long as the picnickers paid for beer or soft drinks to go along with their meals. There was always plenty of music for the visitors' pleasure as well. In the early days, there were gambling, shell games and other questionable enterprises being carried on at the beach.

## Staten Island

By 1890, South Beach had been reformed. It no longer had any games of chance or the *fakirs* (cheats) who ran them. The beach acquired newly painted and varnished bathing kiosks. Strolling photographers did a brisk business by charging fair prices. The women running the bathing kiosks were very pleasant and offered to throw in stockings to anyone who purchased one of their striped bathing suits.

Beer gardens were separated from the beach by a new boardwalk. The resort had become popular not only with Manhattanites and Brooklynites, who arrived before breakfast on hot mornings, but also with Staten Islanders, who came by train with their large bathing parties. The *Press* tells a story about how parents gave their children sand baths at South Beach. The children were buried in rows in the sand with only their heads sticking out. They were then subjected to the "douche." The douche was a shower at the beach. South Beach had many douches. Everyone from children to adults used them to rinse off after spending time at the beach. Children often left the douche and rolled in the sand, so they would have to run the gauntlet of the douche again.

By one o'clock in the afternoon, the whole nature of the beach changed. The visitors migrated to the beer gardens with their picnic baskets, and the

parties began. Hundreds of tables filled up with the picnickers. Everyone drank their beer from earthen mugs and enjoyed the mandolin and piano music. The frankfurter man sold his wares to the hungry people on the boardwalk. The crowd consisted of families with their children, along with young women and men.

In 1899, LaMarcus Adna Thompson and James A. Griffiths built a scenic railroad at South Beach. Although the ride was gone in four years, it marked a new beginning for bigger attractions at the beach.

In September 1896, one of many fires that ravaged South Beach destroyed seven hotels and several small businesses. The boardwalk was also badly damaged. Among the damaged buildings were Bauer's Hotel, Mrs. Miller's Hotel, B.J. Dunn's business, the Binis Hotel, the Looff merry-go-round, photograph galleries and two hundred bathhouses owned by the Bauer and Alhambra Hotels. Six hundred feet of the 1,700-foot boardwalk were also destroyed.

The year 1906 marked the beginning of a new era for entertainment at South Beach when Happyland opened on June 30. Happyland was built by the South Beach Amusement Company, a corporation funded in part by the Bachman Brewing Company, the Rubsam & Horrman Brewing Company and the Electric Railway Company. The amusement company invested $250,000 in the park. At the time of the opening, Albert Hergenhan was the general manager. Hergenhan had been the owner of a casino called the Olympia in South Beach dating from the 1890s until a fire destroyed it around the turn of the century. The Olympia's vaudeville shows usually included seven or eight acts. The show always closed with the biggest act, called *Living Pictures*. This was a presentation of staged scenes in which groups of young women posed clad only in flesh-colored tights. Visitors to the Olympia always stayed to see this show even if it meant having to travel home on overcrowded trolleys and boats.

Happyland was a full-scale amusement park with 1,000 feet of beach and a 30-foot-wide boardwalk in front of it. The park was enclosed and contained natural groves and picnic areas, Japanese tea gardens, a gigantic water-operated circle swing, a Magnetic House (which was a walk-through house of illusion), an airship, a carousel, the Foolish House, a scenic railroad built by the L.A. Thompson Company, a miniature railroad constructed by the Cagney Brothers, shoot-the-chutes and a 190-foot revolving tower.

Bolosy Kiralfy's show, *A Carnival of Venice*, was presented in a specially designed theater. The open-air venue seated three thousand with a stage that was three hundred feet long. The show advertised in the *New York Times*

Bolosy Kiralfy's *Carnival of Venice* played during Happyland's first year in 1906. *Courtesy of Bob Stonehill.*

that its three hundred performers were dressed in "superlatively gorgeous costumes." Gleaming water reproduced the Grand Canal of Venice. The show "for continuous months set all great London agog with entranced amazement and delight." In addition to this theater, there was a vaudeville theater that ran continuous shows, a ballroom and a bandstand. A ten-cent admission was charged for all visitors.

In addition to the major attractions, the park had penny arcades, shooting galleries, a roller-skating rink and many restaurants, including one with a roof garden. Happyland was lit by tens of thousands of lights. A pier 1,500 feet long led directly to the entrance of Happyland.

On June 30, 1906, the first day the park was opened, it was estimated that thirty thousand people attended. No admission was charged. Unfortunately, a storm prevented the *Carnival of Venice* show from making its debut since part of the stage was exposed. Visitors had plenty of shelter in the vaudeville theater and the ballroom, so despite the storm, the opening was deemed a success.

The *New York Times* reported on August 5, 1906, that all of Staten Island was thrown into darkness by a power failure. Happyland was the exception. The Richmond Light and Railroad Company used all of the electricity it generated to power the thousands of lights at Happyland. By the following day, the conditions had not improved. Some trolleys were running, but once again all the lights were bright in Happyland.

Victor D. Levitt became the general manager of Happyland in 1907. In 1915, he became the president of his own business, the Victor Amusement Company, which had its offices at 1402 Broadway in New York City. He became the first chairman of the National Outdoor Showmen Association (NOSA) when it was formed in 1916. Levitt spent his career in entertainment, forming several companies along the way, including Levitt-Meyerhoff Shows United, Levitt-Huggins Greater Allied Shows and, later, Levitt-Taxier Shows United. These companies provided first-rate vaudeville acts throughout the United States.

Under Levitt's management, admission to the park provided not only free band concerts but also free access to vaudeville shows. A newly enlarged ballroom, a skating rink and other new attractions appeared. Opening week featured a free circus ring in the Hippodrome with the Five Flying Gordons performing their daring aerial feats. Latina, the physical culture girl, and Gourney, Keenan and Gourney, an acrobatic act that appeared in *Bumping the Bumps*, also performed. Levitt also brought another show to the park called *Joseph Ferari's Animal Show*. It featured Princess Wiona, Thelma's lions, Irwin's educated dogs, Brown's educated seals, Sebastian's educated ponies, India Zenoa's leopards, lions, pumas, jaguars, bears and boarhounds. This show was accompanied by music from a Gavioli organ. The park also featured a fire show called *The Firemen's Christmas Eve*.

Later in the season, entertainment was provided by gymnast Mlle. Martha, Rae and Benedetto's revolving ladder, the Epps-Loretta Troupe and Alfreno, a high-wire walker in the German Village. A large carousel replaced the theater where Kiralfy's show had run the previous year at the south end of Happyland. A new free picnic area and playground for children were set in a grove of fruit trees.

Levitt created a new concept when he gave visitors a "pass-out check." This check allowed visitors to leave the park and return free of charge. It eventually became common at many parks.

In June 1907, several people were arrested in Staten Island for violating the Sunday Blue Laws. Police Inspector Hogan kept a promise made to the ministers of Richmond to enforce these laws. Several people were given warnings, but George Schaeffer, who was looking to test the law, and six baseball players were arrested for playing baseball on Sunday. Victor Levitt and Thelma Larkin, a lion tamer from Happyland, were also arrested for performing on a Sunday. Twenty others were taken into custody for selling popcorn, peanuts and other items on the boardwalk.

For ten days in June 1907, Lincoln Beachy, the daring aeronaut, made two flights a day from the grounds of Happyland aboard his "airship."

Lincoln was a pioneer during the early era of aviation. Not only did he fly balloons, but he also flew one-man dirigibles, biplanes and monoplanes. His career lasted ten years, from 1905 to 1915, when he was killed during a flying exposition in San Francisco in one of his monoplanes. His airship at Happyland was a fifty-two-foot-long by sixteen-foot-wide balloon with a propeller at one end and a rudder at the other to control its direction.

During one of his flights from Happyland, Lincoln wanted to outdo himself, so he flew over Fort Wadsworth in Staten Island and dropped free tickets to Happyland for the soldiers stationed there. He then flew across the bay and circled over Brooklyn before turning back and landing in Battery Park. A crowd of onlookers rushed to the balloon and broke the propeller, unbeknownst to Lincoln. The police were called to control the gathering crowd, and Lincoln was told he had to leave the park quickly or be arrested. He thought of going to Central Park but was warned if he did so, the police would be there and would arrest him on his arrival.

Lincoln took off with the intention of flying up to Twenty-third Street and around the Flatiron Building before returning to Happyland. As he flew, he noticed that the propeller was making a loud knocking sound. He killed the engine, fearing that if a piece of the propeller broke off, it could rip a hole in the balloon.

He was totally at the mercy of an easterly flowing wind. Beachy found himself flying over the East River near Little Hell Gate and Randall's Island. He decided to bring the balloon down. He saw a lighthouse and a small buoy in the river and started to let some air out of the balloon to land there. The balloon hit the lighthouse, which ripped a hole in its side and sent it onto the point of the buoy. Fortunately for him, a flotilla of boats had been following his progress. He was rescued with no harm done to him except for wet feet. Lincoln and his balloon were loaded onto Captain "Bill" Churchill's sloop, *Easy Times*, and they all sailed back to Happyland. Lincoln still had four or five more days at Happyland. He made plans to repair his balloon so he could continue the daily flights, but not to Manhattan.

By July 1907, Happyland was drawing weekend crowds in excess of twenty thousand. Every week, a new vaudeville show was performed in the German Village. On July 11, 1907, a baby contest was held at Happyland with a number of categories offering a prize for each. Other events included a carnival for schoolchildren, held from September 9 to September 14. Not only were $500 in prizes offered, but also more than three thousand boxes of candy were given out to the children. Mr. Levitt, the manager of Happyland, invited children from the New York Orphan's Home at Hastings-on-Hudson to Happyland for a day of entertainment.

Charles Henderson and Fred M. Schubert brought a Chinese theater show to Happyland, claiming it was the only real Chinese show outside Peking. The show featured the Hop Sing Tong performing Chinese vaudeville, a Chinese wedding, singers and dancers, an opium den, religious ceremonies and a band of Chinese musicians. Capacity crowds filled every performance. Henderson and Schubert planned to take the show on the road after Happyland closed for the season.

Albert Hergenhan took over the park's management in 1909, and he made it a free park. By 1914, there were numerous attractions on the boardwalk at South Beach besides the self-contained Happyland. Four photograph studios, a shooting gallery, a horoscope and "tells the name" stand, the Aquehonga Dance Hall, a bowling alley, a souvenir shop, a card-printing stand, a Japanese ball-rolling game, a dance hall, a cane rack and a cane game provided plenty of variety for the throngs.

In addition, there were rides on the boardwalk, including Henry Tirelli's carousel (Philadelphia Toboggan Company's PTC #14), with its new $5,000 Berni organ. The Berni Organ Company was one of the foremost makers of mechanical organs being used in the amusement ride industry at the time. A second carousel run by Murphy and Nunley was entering its eighth year of service on the boardwalk near Happyland.

Screams and laughs were heard from the Roller Boller Coaster built by James A. Griffiths and L.A. Thompson. Griffiths and Thompson also built a second coaster called the Dips, which ran at South Beach from 1907 to 1917.

Of course, any destination dependent on transportation to deliver its visitors has a problem when that transportation system fails. In August 1916, the workers of the Richmond Light and Railroad Company went on strike, stranding twenty thousand people at South and Midland Beaches. Many people made the four-mile walk from the beach to the Municipal Ferry at Saint George, but many more stayed behind. Hundreds of men and boys slept on the beach. The railroad workers wanted a raise of five cents an hour, from twenty-five cents to thirty cents. They also demanded recognition of their union. Management agreed to the raise but was hesitant to recognize the union. The strike lasted two days before the railroad company and the workers came to an agreement. The agreement did not allow the workers to organize but gave workers a pay raise. It was agreed that anyone who struck would be treated the same after the strike as before. There was no signed agreement between the railroad company and the union.

# Staten Island

James Griffiths and L.A. Thompson's Roller Boller Coaster was one of several roller coasters that were in Happyland over the years. *Courtesy of Bob Stonehill.*

The worst disaster to strike Happyland occurred on May 4, 1919. The park was completely destroyed by a fire. Flames were first observed at three o'clock in the morning. The blaze very quickly spread, and a general alarm brought out all the fire apparatus on Staten Island. In addition to the park's destruction, adjoining bungalows, Hotel Walnord, Schaerfer's Hotel and Roderick's restaurant were also destroyed. The damage was estimated to be $250,000. Two firemen were injured attempting to extinguish the inferno.

Mrs. Mary Autenreit was burned to death trying to rescue some of her belongings from the fire. Her husband, John, was president of the Bay Amusement Company, which had been planning to operate concessions at the park. The blaze was fanned by high winds and lit up the early morning sky. Hundreds of people went to the shores of Coney Island, Sandy Hook and New Jersey to witness the spectacle.

The boardwalk at South Beach was quickly rebuilt, and some new rides were introduced, including the Dodgem, a bumper car ride operated by Henry Tirelli in the 1920s. But Happyland never regained its status as the great amusement park it had once been. In 1929, a series of suspicious fires was started under the boardwalk on five successive Sundays at around the same time. These fires burned several hotels, bathhouses and the boardwalk once again.

Starting in 1935, when Franklin D. Roosevelt's Works Progress Administration (WPA) began a series of public works projects to provide jobs for Depression-era workers, South Beach began to rejuvenate. One of the projects included the construction of a new two-and-a-half-mile boardwalk from Fort Wadsworth to Sea View. In order to build the boardwalk,

The Philadelphia Toboggan Company's Carousel #14 was built in 1906. It was moved to Happyland in 1912, after its run at Clason Point in the Bronx.

remnants of the old boardwalk and deteriorating music halls, carousels and concessions were removed.

Since 1995, James Molinaro, borough president of Staten Island, allotted $20 million for improvements to the boardwalk and beach area. The northern end featured a new Dolphin Fountain, which became a local meeting point. The southern end (near Midland Beach) featured Freedom Circle, which was dedicated to the men and women who fought for our country's freedom. Young and old were able to enjoy the playgrounds, ballparks and handball courts. The more adventurous could play roller hockey or perform stunts in the skateboard park. Shuffleboard, bocce and checker tables were provided for those who enjoyed more leisurely activities.

In 2002, the Ocean Breeze Fishing Pier was erected. The pier was 835 feet long, making it one of the longest in New York City.

One of the holdovers from the amusement park era remained until 1998, when the property was sold. This was the South Beach Amusement Park, a one-acre playland in the shadow of the Verrazano Bridge. A July 4, 1998 article in the *New York Times* described the state of the park. The park contained sixteen "kiddie" rides: the Jolly Caterpillar, a rocket ship ride, the Tilt-a-Whirl and the Jack Rabbit coaster, among others. Rock music from the 1960s and '70s was played. The park had no shade and was surrounded on two sides by weeds taller than an adult. The rides, too, had seen better days. Some were rusting from lack of maintenance. Tickets were $1.25 per ride, twenty tickets for $20 and forty rides for $35. Though some would find it sad and depressing, the children there seemed to disagree. The second generation of the Lepre family eventually sold the amusement park. The property on Sand Lane in South Beach is now town houses.

Across the street from South Beach Amusement Park was the last holdout, an arcade called Beachland Amusements. Beachland Amusements was established in 1941 on the boardwalk at South Beach. When the city banned commercial establishments from the boardwalk in 1953, the arcade moved across the street from the South Beach Amusement Park. The arcade started out with mechanical games, but the owners, keeping up with the times, moved on to video games as they became popular. When the season ended in 2006, it marked the end of sixty-six years in business. From 2006 until 2011, the arcade remained a shuttered and neglected place. The plans were for the building to become a Key Food supermarket run by a family from Tottenville. Amy and Joseph Doleh planned to be hands-on owners with their three children pitching in to work the counters.

In October 2012, Hurricane Sandy ravaged the Northeast, with Staten Island being particularly hard hit. The storm destroyed most of the boardwalk and the surrounding area. As of this writing (2013), plans are underway to once again rebuild.

## Midland Beach

Midland Beach is on the southeastern shore of Staten Island, about six and a half miles from Saint George. It is the next town down the coast from South Beach. The two towns have a similar history as ocean shore amusement areas. The construction of the ferry terminal in Saint George, along with the expansion of the Staten Island Railway from Saint George to Tottenville in the late 1880s, aided the growth of Staten Island's shoreline. This expansion enticed visitors from Manhattan, Brooklyn and New Jersey to travel to the Staten Island shore for relaxation and entertainment.

By the 1890s, Midland Beach had gained popularity as a summer resort offering cooling ocean breezes, fine bathing, hotels, a casino and a number of excellent restaurants. In May 1898, the informal opening of Midland Beach for the season drew a large crowd to the beach area.

The pier at Midland Beach extended into the bay to allow for fishing and strolling. It was over 1,700 feet long, so a miniature railroad was built to take

visitors out to its end point. The *William Story*, a steamboat that picked up passengers at the Battery in lower Manhattan, brought passengers to the pier at Midland Beach in fifty minutes.

Several jurisdictional disagreements occurred around this time. In September 1900, a fight broke out between the proprietors of Midland Beach and those of Woodland Beach, one town south of Midland. The great Midland pier was located at the southern end of Midland Beach. The

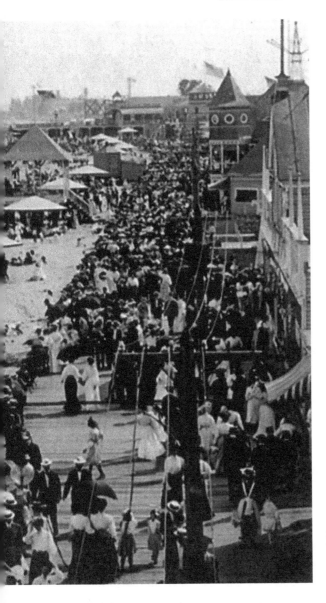

A view of the boardwalk at Midland Beach is shown in 1905. In the distance, one can see the pier stretching out into the bay. *Library of Congress.*

proprietors of Midland Beach constructed a fence at the boardwalk end of the pier that forced visitors from Woodland Beach to walk to the road and go behind the resorts if they wished to travel between the two towns. This was an attempt by Midland Beach proprietors to prevent undesirables from adjacent Woodland Beach from entering their property.

In protest, fifteen residents of Woodland Beach, armed with axes, attempted to chop a hole in the fence to allow themselves passage. Seeing this, the Midland Beach contingent rapidly responded and attempted to take away the axes. Police on the scene stood by but did nothing to stop the destruction of property. They stated that their orders were to ensure that no one was injured in the fracas. Shortly after the mêlée, the barricade was rebuilt on the orders of John Hinchliffe, mayor of Paterson, New Jersey, and president of the Midland Beach Company, the owner of the property.

The barricade was again torn down by Woodland residents. W.H. Putnam, a Woodland Beach proprietor, declared that people wished to come to Woodland Beach because they had their choice of beer and were not limited to Mr. Hinchcliffe's brew. Hinchliffe responded by stating that the fence was built to keep Midland Beach free of the bad elements that went to Woodland Beach. Finally, a truce was called.

By 1904, visitors were flocking to Midland Beach because the destination was one of beauty and orderliness. There were several hotels and thousands of bungalows where families could spend a few days or the entire season. Visitors were rewarded with quiet comfort and many available services. There was nothing to annoy or offend anyone, unlike at other nearby resorts. This set Midland Beach apart from other beaches in the metropolitan area.

There were myriad activities for everyone in the family to enjoy. Fishing from the long Midland Beach pier was a popular diversion for men. Men and women could also enjoy sitting on the boardwalk, enjoying the sun and breezes as they listened to the free orchestra concerts offered three times a day.

For those who preferred strolling, there were several miles of white sandy beach on which the tides left a variety of shells and interesting driftwood. Swimming at the beach was safe since there was very little undertow to catch the unwary bather. The beach had dozens of toadstool-shaped shelters to accommodate the large numbers of picnickers. These shelters could be used free of charge. Picnicking was encouraged largely because shrewd beer and other concession owners realized the spin-off profit potential.

The Aquarama delighted people of all ages with its panoramic scenic views. One could test his skill at Japanese bowling or enjoy a light snack at one of the small kiosks on the boardwalk.

For those who were more adventurous, there was the Ferris wheel and L.A. Thompson's Scenic Railway. Thompson's railway had been one of the attractions at the Pan-American Exposition held in Buffalo, New York, in 1901. It was disassembled and transported to Midland Beach shortly after the exposition's closing. A dance pavilion provided fine music and an excellent dance floor on which to dance the day and evening away. Midland

One of the staples of early amusements was the circle swing. The carriers were sometimes simple swings, airplanes or boats. *Courtesy of Bob Stonehill.*

Beach boasted a carousel built by Charles I.D. Looff and a circle swing with carriers shaped like small boats.

Around sundown, the view across the bay to Coney Island provided visitors with a panorama of illumination and color. When fireworks at Coney Island lit the night sky, they were clearly visible from Midland Beach as well. Besides the view across the water, the illuminated boardwalk, hotels, restaurants and attractions all added greatly to the lights and color at the beach.

The Midland Beach Theatre, operated by T.K. Albaugh, provided vaudeville and comic opera every evening at 8:15 p.m., in addition to Saturday matinees. The bill of fare was changed weekly to provide a variety of entertainment. To encourage women and children to attend, alcohol was prohibited in the theater. Such a policy was designed to ensure a healthy family atmosphere at the shows.

Fires were major problems for all resorts and amusement areas at the time, and Midland Beach did not escape their wrath. There were several fires over the years. In September 1916, a grease fire that started in Michael's Restaurant quickly spread to nearby bungalows and homes along the beachfront. A bucket brigade was formed as pails of water were passed from the bay in an attempt to douse the flames. Sparks from the fire blanketed the beach, where three thousand tents had been pitched by New Yorkers summering at Midland Beach. Many of these tents were destroyed. The damage was estimated at $10,000. After the fire was extinguished, it was discovered that the electric plant no longer worked. People left the beach in darkness searching for the trolley tracks to take them back to Saint George. Several people lost their way in the dark and had to be rescued by policemen with oil lamps.

After each fire gutted sections of the resort, the proprietors rebuilt the damaged or destroyed properties, which included hotels, summer bungalows, sections of the boardwalk, portions of the pier and the amusements. Over the years, many older amusement rides were replaced by newer ones as they were damaged or as newer ones came into vogue.

The park had three different roller coasters at different times in its history. L.A. Thompson's Scenic Railway closed in 1924. The Giant Coaster built by Arthur Jarvis came along around 1921, and finally the Whirlwind Racer, designed by Harry G. Traver, operated from 1929 to 1935. All of these coasters were constructed of wood.

Any venue offering amusement rides feared accidents, and Midland Beach was not immune. In August 1917, a man toppled from a coaster car and was hurled toward the ground fifty feet below. The man had been standing in the coaster as it reached the top of a loop. Fortunately for him, his right foot got caught in the wooden structure, preventing him from falling to his death. Rescuers accidentally broke his leg while trying to extricate him. It took firemen from New Dorp a half hour to finally bring the man down from his precarious position.

Another accident occurred on July 6, 1918, shortly after 8:00 p.m., when the circle swing collapsed and fell to the ground. Fortunately, the injuries were only minor. Several people suffered bruises, scratches or minor contusions. Everyone who was treated was able to return home that night.

On June 28 and 29, 1918, Midland Beach held a carnival and charged admission for the first time. The admission charge of ten cents was donated to the Red Cross. The carnival was sponsored by the Midland Beach Branch of the Civic League of Staten Island. John Hinchliffe and all the other show managers donated 25 percent of their gross income to the Red Cross as well. Several vaudeville acts volunteered their time to perform for these shows. A dance contest was also held. The event started with a parade led by the Staten Island borough president, Van Name, and included soldiers, sailors, Boy Scouts, marines and Red Cross workers. It was estimated that a crowd of well over ten thousand attended opening night of the carnival.

# Staten Island

The pier at Midland Beach was so long that a miniature train was used to bring visitors to its end. *Courtesy of Bob Stonehill.*

The summer of 1923 brought the largest crowds ever up to that point to Staten Island. It was estimated that at least 150,000 people came to the island on June 24, 1923. Most of them went to either Midland or South Beach. By 2:00 p.m., vendors were out of sandwiches, confections and soft drinks. When the crowd started leaving at dusk, a major problem was created. The six Staten Island municipal ferries could not accommodate all the passengers and automobiles waiting to return to Manhattan. By midnight, hundreds of automobiles still waited on line for the ferries. The line of cars, three abreast, stretched from Saint George to Tompkinsville, a mile away. Finally, the Thirty-ninth Street Municipal Ferry from Manhattan sent two additional boats to help with the overload of people and automobiles.

Another incident occurred on July 4, 1923. A tremendous storm hit Staten Island, and lightning struck two buildings, igniting a large fire. Between twenty-five and thirty thousand people at Midland and South Beaches went into a panic trying to find shelter on the boardwalk. The municipal trolleys could not run because some of their tracks were washed out. In addition, the high wind brought down many electric lines, leaving sections of the beaches in darkness. Once the storm ended, the crush of people heading home created yet another serious problem for the municipal ferries and trolleys. Police were sent out, once again with oil lamps, to help locate visitors who got lost in the dark trying to find their return trip transportation.

In 1924, the owners of Midland Beach opened a saltwater pool, which was advertised as "the largest salt water pool on the east coast." It should be noted that most amusement-area concessionaires were subject to hyperbole, and many made similar claims.

A nearly fatal blow to the Midland Beach resort and amusement area came on August 7, 1924. Two fires broke out on the Midland Beach pier. The first fire started on the west end of the pier and was quickly extinguished. The firemen had no sooner returned to their station after dousing the fire when a second one broke out. This secondary blaze nearly destroyed the great pier. Damage was estimated to be $5,000. The pier had been used not only by visitors enjoying the festivities but also by the Midland Beach Amusement Association as docking space for its boats.

The Midland Beach resort and amusement area closed for the season, in its crippled state, on September 13, 1924. A few weeks later, on September 26, 1924, a major fire swept through the resort and left it in ruins. The first flames were seen by a watchman in a carousel building. The blaze was quickly called in. By the time the first fire apparatus arrived, the blaze had become a three-alarm fire. The fire rapidly spread to the roller coaster, and it became apparent that the resort was doomed. The summer bungalow colony of nearly five thousand bungalows was threatened by the flames, but the firemen were able to save them.

At the height of the fire, it became an all-borough alarm, and eventually fire stations in Manhattan were asked to aid as well. The Staten Island fireboat *Zohar Mills*, along with two other fireboats, pumped water on the fire from the bay while firemen pumped water from fire hydrants. As the hydrants were few and far between, enormous lengths of hose were needed to reach the flames. It took over three hours before the blaze was brought under control.

By the time it was over, four hotels, fifteen bungalows, the Midland Beach pier and a number of small businesses were destroyed. Additional structures destroyed included the toboggan slide, the Witching Waves attraction, a carousel, the Ferris wheel, the Old Homestead Restaurant, the Richmond Hotel, Cable's Hotel, the bathing pavilion, the Dunlea Hotel dance club and restaurant and several small stores. The most imposing structure on the beach, the Midland Beach Hotel, which was five stories high and contained 450 rooms, was razed as well. In addition, the concrete home of the park's manager, William Leonard, was destroyed, and part of a concrete path three-quarters of a mile long was ruined.

The damage was estimated at $750,000. Due to high premiums, very little of the property had been covered by insurance. The largest concession was still

A couple of bathing beauties pose on Midland Beach in front of an airplane ride.

owned by the Midland Beach Amusement Company and its president, William Hinchliffe. The Hinchliffe family had owned the property for thirty years.

In 1925, James S. Graham bought most of the property at Midland Beach from the Hinchliffe family. His plan was to unite Woodland Beach, Midland Beach and Graham Beach into one contiguous beach with a mile and a quarter beachfront. By 1929, after Graham had rebuilt Midland Beach with an Old Mill, a Barrel of Fun, a scenic railroad, skee ball alleys and myriad other amusements, the scourge of yet another fire erupted and burned down a quarter of the park. The great saltwater pool was also damaged in the fire. Management estimated the damage to be between $250,000 and $300,000. Daniel Leonard, the manager of Midland Beach at that time, felt the damage could be repaired in time for the June 1, 1929 opening.

After the fire, Midland Beach limped along with few large amusement attractions left. It was mainly used for swimming and sunbathing at the beach and pool. For several years, canoe races were held offshore near Midland

Beach. The beach became restricted, wherein visitors were required to pay a charge of twenty-five cents to use the beach and pool facilities.

In 1934, the New York City Board of Estimate adopted a resolution to change the city map so that a public beach running for two and a half miles from South Beach to Midland Beach would be included. In turn, this would make the beach free to the public once again.

When Franklin D. Roosevelt began his Works Progress Administration in 1935, $1,092,961 was allotted for the construction of a new boardwalk along Staten Island's south shore. The plan included clearing rocks from the beach and extending it so that at least 250 feet of beach would be available at high tide. The project would employ up to four thousand men.

The City of New York spent $6,460,000 in 1954 to once again improve the beaches from South Beach to Graham Beach. The cost included demolition of old, dilapidated structures; adding bathhouses, parking lots and comfort stations; and repairing the boardwalk. The area contained playgrounds, ballparks and handball courts. In addition, there were roller hockey and skateboard parks. Shuffleboard, bocce and checker tables were available as well.

Just as in the case of South Beach, Hurricane Sandy dealt a near fatal blow to Midland Beach. Tentative plans call for rebuilding.

# 3
# BROOKLYN

## GOLDEN CITY

The Canarsie section of Brooklyn is located in the borough's southeastern part, nestled between Flatlands and East New York. At the southernmost end of Canarsie lies Jamaica Bay. The Canarsie Pier extends into the bay and serves as a recreational area under the auspices of the National Park Service. Today, Canarsie is primarily a residential area of single- and two-family homes with a distinct Caribbean flavor. Its population is just under 100,000.

But like so many New York City neighborhoods, it has undergone many transformations. Before the first European settlers arrived, Native Americans (the Canarsees) harvested the bay for shellfish. This food bounty provided sustenance, but the natives also used the remnant shells to fashion polished beads that were strung and used as wampum. The Dutch settled Canarsie in 1636, making it the oldest settlement on Long Island (including Brooklyn, Queens, Nassau and Suffolk) and the second oldest in the tri-state area. Only settlements in Manhattan date back further.

After the Dutch arrived, the native population began to dwindle dramatically. In 1665, the Dutch purchased the land they had settled from the local tribes. Their "price" was some trinkets, alcohol and several items of clothing. The bay area continued to support a thriving fishing industry as the oysters, clams, fish and even lobsters were highly valued. But around 1920, the city banned commercial fishing in the bay as a result of polluted waters. Starting in the 1930s, Canarsie was becoming an Italian American working-class area.

To trace the development of Golden City Park, one needs to look back in time. By 1860, Canarsie's population was still modest (about three thousand), but its emergence as a resort area would change its course forever. Steam trains were delivering thirty thousand visitors annually to the shore area by this time. Over fifty hotels, many along Avenue L, serviced this transient population. Resorts at Bergen Beach, Brighton Beach, Rockaway and Coney Island sprang up. The colossal success of Coney Island's amusements around the turn of the century made it a nationwide and, arguably, worldwide sensation. Entrepreneurs saw the potential to lure some of Coney Island's customers their way. They were quick to respond.

Around the turn of the twentieth century, a park's location was crucial. In addition to the rides and other amusements, urban dwellers sought relief from the sweltering summer days. Locations near populated areas bordered by natural bodies of water were considered prime since they provided the scenic and cooling effects desired. Public transportation needed to be convenient since the automobile had not yet become available to the masses.

The Traver Circle Swing Company of 66 Broadway in Manhattan took an interest in the project and saw the potential on the bay at Canarsie. The company was a premier amusement ride builder. Its good fortunes began with the construction of large circle swings, a staple in many parks. It extended its interests by developing and producing other amusement rides. Highly successful, it parlayed its gains by buying and operating entire parks in the United States, Canada and Europe.

It is unclear what ultimate role the Traver Circle Swing Company played in the construction and operation of Golden City Park because an individual named William J. Warner Jr. came along and expressed an interest in the project as well. Warner is generally associated with Golden City Park's early years, and his involvement with Golden City Park will be discussed later. But there is little question that, at the very least, the Traver Circle Swing Company was involved in the development of the plans for the attractions and the park's layout and construction. The company took out a full-page advertisement in *Billboard*, appearing on November 24, 1906 (some six months before the projected opening day), announcing that it was building Golden City, "the most stupendous achievement in amusement park construction yet attempted." It projected that two million visitors could access the park for only a five-cent fare (Coney Island was a double fare for most people and fifteen cents for those coming from the east side of

# GOLDEN CITY

## The Most Stupendous Achievement in Amusement Park Construction Yet Attempted.

### ☛ A TRIUMPH IN CLASSIC ARCHITECTURE

All of the beauties from the imposing Acropolis of Athens, the world famed Alhambra of Spain, the wonderful Pantheon of Rome, and other notable masterpieces of the world's builders have been availed of to dazzle the amusement lover in the Golden City.

### TWO MILLION PEOPLE WITHIN 5 CENTS FARE.

This greatest of all amusement parks is being built on Canarsie Shore, New York City, by the Traver Circle Swing Co. The location is ideal, being a clear and level piece of ground fronting on Jamaica Bay. It forms the entire property surrounding the terminus of two street car lines, three steamboat lines and an elevated railroad. All of these lines reach the most densely populated tenement-house districts of the north side of Brooklyn and the east side of New York. Forty-two lines of surface cars and seven elevated railroads transfer free to the Golden City cars, thus bringing two million people within a five cent fare and a half hour's ride of the great resort. The Golden City is the first big amusement park established within a five cent fare of Manhattan. It is the first great park to be built in New York City, outside of Coney Island. Never before in the history of amusements has an amusement park been built within five cent fare of such a tremendous population.

### FOUR YEARS' PREPARATION.

For four years the Traver Circle Swing Co. has been building and operating Circle Swings and other amusements in the best resorts in the United States, Canada and Europe. During all this time ideas and plans were being quietly collected and prepared for the building of an amusement park. There was no hurry, no waste, no extravagance, no partially matured plans. The building and operation of other resorts were watched carefully. Successes and failures were noted. The wise and foolish expenditures were tabulated and the good and bad results of advertising methods were weighed in the balance. Four trips to Europe were made for the purpose of studying the architectural wonders of the old world and for the purpose of collecting up-to-date amusement novelties. Nothing was too good for this great venture. Never before was so much time, labor and money spent in mere preparation for such an undertaking.

The climax of all this preparation was reached with the selection of the site. No matter how great the preparation nor how well laid out the plans, these would avail nothing if the park were not located in a favorable spot. Many sites were inspected, all of which were more or less promising, but all of these paled into insignificance when compared with Canarsie. It was thought that no site should be considered without a two million population near, and that every modern facility must be had for transporting tremendous throngs. The car fare should not be more than five cents. A site on the water front was preferred, to give facilities for boating and other aquatic sports. A site was preferred also where people do not have access to other resorts. Canarsie meets all these requirements exactly. Coney Island is a ten cent fare and seventy minutes ride from the north side of Brooklyn; and it is a fifteen cent fare and an hour-and-a-half ride from the east side of Manhattan. Coney Island and Canarsie do not compete in any way whatever. The Traver Circle Swing Co. have taken a long lease on the entire property, and there can be NO OTHER AMUSEMENTS OUTSIDE OF THE GOLDEN CITY.

### PLANNED FROM EXPERIENCE.

The main entrance will be modeled after the Arco della Pace of Milan, Italy, with an imposing colonade extending for two hundred feet on either side. The grand promenade will be laid out in the form of a great crescent, facing the sea, the horns of which will be tipped with two great casinos built on piers over the water. One of these will be used as a skating rink and the other as a dance hall. The promenade will be covered by a Greek colonade with Corinthian columns, so that patrons of the park may visit all of the attractions fronting on the promenade without exposure to sun or rain. The material used will be wood, steel and cement, but no staff will be used, as it is not sufficiently durable. The entire park will be treated with a new process resembling white marble, and the only colors will be white and gold; hence the name GOLDEN CITY.

### SPECIAL FREE SHOWS.

A feature of operation will be a series of great out-door acts and other special attractions, which will be extensively advertised to increase the patronage. A contract has been made, providing for $45,000 worth of such attractions. On one night each week a gorgeous display of fireworks will be made from a float in the Bay in full view of all patrons of the park. An expert is now booking outings and picnics for every day of the week except Saturday and Sunday, thereby increasing the business during the usual dull period. New York has 5,000,000 people, and this class of business has never been catered to before.

### GREAT NEW ATTRACTION.

The chief amusement feature for 1907 will be a magnificent Electro-Mechanical Scenic Production entitled "Robinson Crusoe," costing $60,000. This wonderful attraction will be housed in an immense building occupying a central position at the rear of the park. It will have a frontage of 120 feet, and the central portion of the roof will be supported by steel arches of 100 feet span. On either side of the entrance to this building will be a magnificent electric tower 90 feet high.

### EVERY SHOW A WINNER.

Among other features which will be built and operated by the company are "Over the Rockies," "Temple of Wonders," Penny Arcade, "Down the Niagara," Miniature Railway, Improved Traver Circle Swing, Excursion Launch, "The Shrine of Sinners," Figure Eight Toboggan, Hale's Tours and a number of smaller attractions. A few Concessions will be let out to desirable parties for the operation of a Shooting Gallery, Photograph Gallery, Refreshment Booths, Carousel and other minor attractions. Applications will be received and space allotted immediately to people who can deliver the goods and make satisfactory terms.

### NOVELTIES WANTED.

The Golden City desires to purchase Novelties with good drawing power and reasonable earning capacity.

The Traver Circle Swing Co. approach the Golden City proposition with the same spirit which they have manifested in the extension of their business throughout the world, and it is thought that a company that can successfully build and operate more than one hundred large amusement plants in a short period of four seasons will make a success of this park, which will eclipse anything heretofore attained.

## TRAVER CIRCLE SWING CO.,
### 66 Broadway, NEW YORK.

The Traver Circle Swing Company placed this advertisement in *Billboard* on November 24, 1906. Golden City Park opened about six months later.

Manhattan). It went on to state that the nine-and-a-half-acre site was clear, level and fronted the bay, making its location ideal. Even on opening day, Traver Circle Swing Company was named as "owner" of the park in several trade publications. It was not until late July 1907 that William J. Warner's company, the Canarsie Amusement Company, took full interest in the park, as will be discussed later.

The park would be serviced by two streetcar lines, three steamship lines and an extension of the "el" to Canarsie Landing. In researching the attractions and the park's architecture, four trips to Europe were undertaken. Planning took four years. Estimates for the total expenditure to build the park varied wildly, but a tab close to $1 million would seem about the average. The land was leased for twenty years from the Brooklyn Canarsie Realty Company. Construction of the park began in September 1906.

Architecturally, the park would have influences from Greece and Italy, among others. The park was laid out in the outline of a crescent facing the sea. Its main entrance was an arch designed after the Arco della Pace of Milan, Italy. The seventy-foot-tall structure was adorned with sculptures of Ben Hur's famous chariot ride. The arch, adorned with lights, was situated near the middle of a colonnade that ran eight hundred feet on the east side of the complex. The colonnade also provided protection for visitors from rain or boiling sun.

At the park's southernmost end, a 25- by 300-foot promenade (or boardwalk) was constructed. It was a Greek-inspired colonnade with Corinthian columns supporting the canopy. The two "anchors" of the promenade on either side were almost identical grand structures built on piers extending into the bay. Both structures were designed after a beautiful casino in Nice, France. The western building would become the dance hall. Its eastern counterpart became the skating rink. They each measured 80 feet by 150 feet, certainly large enough to accommodate several thousand dancers and skaters.

The park's theme colors were white and gold (hence "Golden City"). The walls and most other painted surfaces were treated with a special German-engineered painting process. Once several coats of the paint were applied, the effect was that of white marble. Over 140,000 lights created a dazzling display of illumination after dusk.

A visitor entering through the park's arch walked across a path covered with crushed clam and oyster shells brought in from Jamaica Bay. Directly ahead stood the bandstand. Free concerts were provided several times a day. Just beyond the stand was a circle swing built by the Traver Circle

Swing Company. The swing could spin forty-eight thrilled riders at a time. The company claimed the swing was the largest in the world. To the left of the bandstand was the circus ring, where free shows were provided all day long. To its right was an electric fountain. Beyond this "inner ring," the larger attractions were situated around the semicircle. Minor attractions were interspersed throughout the park, as were countless refreshment and souvenir stalls.

Theater and vaudeville were mainstays of entertainment during this time. Thompson and Dundy's Hippodrome in Manhattan set the gold standard. Finished in 1905, it is still considered an architectural wonder. Its presentations were immediately successful, and its 5,300 seats were filled to capacity for most performances. Its first staging was a two-act extravaganza. The first act, "A Yankee Circus on Mars," featured spaceships, elephants, horses, a sixty-piece orchestra and several hundred singers and dancers. In contrast to that fantasy, the second act of the four-hour show *Andersonville* portrayed a noted Civil War military prison where many Union soldiers were maltreated. Bouts of gunfire and explosions startled the audience. A giant pool was constructed to simulate the camp's lake.

Golden City Park countered with its Golden City Theater. The theater's cost estimates ranged from $40,000 to $60,000. It was an immense structure set at the rear and center of the park. It had a frontage of 120 feet. Standing sentinel at either side of the theater were twin towers, each soaring 140 feet. Seven thousand lights adorned the outline of the beautiful building. It seated in excess of 2,500 patrons.

The first production at the theater was *Robinson Crusoe*, described as an "electrical-mechanical scenic production." There were five scenes depicting the title hero's travails. The opening scene showed Crusoe sailing from home. This was followed by scene changes highlighting the vessel at sea, the great storm, the shipwreck off the island of Terra del Fuego and, finally, the rescue of Crusoe and his man Friday by a passing ship. Fourteen giant electric motors were needed to move the sixty thousand square feet of scenery during the presentation. Warner, after he assumed control of the park's operations, paid $60,000 for the rights to the production for two years. The show had been a huge success in Brighton, England. *Robinson Crusoe* was promoted as the show that would surpass any production in the country. Unfortunately, no reviews have been found to back that claim.

Another feature attraction was the scenic waterway "Down the Niagara." After one entered the building through a huge arch, he was met by a huge replica of Niagara Falls. No doubt, visitors were refreshed by the ensuing

This artist's rendition of the Golden City Theater shows the front façade with its twin 140-foot towers. *Robinson Crusoe* was the park's first production.

ride down the rapids as they enjoyed the story of Hiawatha. The "Temple of Wonders" was imported from Austria. It was billed as "a most wonderful collection of European novelties; marvels never seen before in America." "Love's Journey" was a novelty ride that had been a big success at Boston's Wonderland Park the previous year. Its cars passed through a dark, circular tunnel when suddenly they were mechanically "flipped" to an outside circle. The ensuing jostling and bouncing created waves of laughter. Men frequently reported losing pocket watches and other items on the topsy-turvy ride. At the ride's end, passengers were showered with confetti blown by electric fans. The whirling voyage was built by Patte-Stedman. The "Live Fox Chase" provided another unique attraction.

The realistic "Forest Fire" was a spectacular reenactment displaying firefighters' techniques as they battled forest blazes. The outrageous "Human Laundry" ride was exactly that. People in bathing attire were "washed" in a giant tub and dried in a spinner. Then, forceful fans would complete the drying job until they were propelled down the laundry chute to the exit.

An electric scenic railway called "Over the Rockies" took its passengers on a chilling third-rail ride through the snow-covered Rocky Mountains.

Designed by Hunter and Rarick, the ride was over 4,200 feet long and was an entirely new attraction to the amusement industry. One of its scenes, "The Grand Canyon of the Colorado," was 75 feet long, 45 feet wide and 40 feet deep. Other scenes included Pike's Peak and a forest fire with flaming pine trees. Another attraction, the "Coliseum" roller coaster, brought its own chills to riders with its unique turns.

Opening "live" acts included King Pharaoh the educated horse. King Pharaoh amazed visitors with his equine intelligence. He was an attraction at the World's Fair in St. Louis. The large Arabian stallion could read, write, tell colors, do arithmetic and perform scores of other feats. While not performing, the horse could be seen "handing out" pictures of himself at his stall. King Pharaoh was owned, taught and trained by Dr. D.B. Boyd of Columbia, South Carolina. The Flying Lady, Okuni Sami, astounded her audiences with illusions that had made her a favorite at Luna Park in Cleveland. A four-horned goat, claimed to be the only one in captivity, amused young and old.

The Truscott Boat Company's *Golden Hour* boat provided some relief from the crowded and hot midways. The naphtha-powered craft whisked sixty passengers at a time through Jamaica Bay as passengers enjoyed the breezes and the bay's salt spray.

Of course, there were a variety of rides and attractions that were staples to most parks back in the day. In addition to the giant circle swing, folks could enjoy a figure-eight toboggan ride, a $10,000 Harton carousel, a Ferris wheel, an Old Mill, Cagney's miniature railway, another coaster, penny arcades (with two hundred machines), McCullogh's shooting gallery, Gale's moving picture show, games of chance and nickelodeons, to name just a few.

Food of all varieties was available, including nickel hot dogs. Those on a tight budget could still enjoy a day at Golden City. Free weekly fireworks displays lit up the night sky from the bay some three hundred feet from the promenade. The free circus acts and concerts could be enjoyed. There were picnic areas set aside for those who brought their own meals. The bay and promenade provided refreshing breezes.

An opening date for Golden City Park was scheduled for the beginning of May 1907, an early start for many parks. Even though construction began in September 1906, seven hundred workers were still on site in February. Time was running short to get all attractions up and running. Attraction buildings were still being built, and flooring was not yet set on the dance floor and skating rink. Lights were still being strung, among a long list of other unfinished items. Three hundred carpenters, painters and others were still toiling as of May 5. Mechanics and scenic artists were behind schedule for the completion of the *Robinson Crusoe* spectacular.

A rescheduled opening for May 18 was also canceled. Concessionaires were still being solicited in the trade magazines. Simultaneously, hotels, restaurants and sideshows were being built just outside Golden City's walls hoping to capitalize on spin-off business. The long-anticipated opening day was pushed back to May 31 due not only to unfinished work but also to unseasonable weather. With expectations to challenge the vaunted Luna Park and Dreamland at Coney Island, the day of reckoning finally arrived. Golden City Park opened its gates to the public on May 31, 1907.

Depending on to whom you spoke or where you read it, the opening day reviews were mixed. The *New York Times* shrugged off the fact that some attractions were not up and running. The Golden City Theater production was not quite ready to open when the gates opened, but to everyone's surprise, the theater's doors flew open about one o'clock in the afternoon. The "Down the Niagara" attraction was not running. The Flying Lady's stage was still being constructed. The newspaper declared that most visitors seemed to be having a wonderful time despite the ongoing construction. King Pharaoh and the miniature railroad drew long lines of parents with children in tow. The coasters and the "Over the Rockies" ride experienced similar backups, as did the carousels, the circle swing and the Ferris wheel. The bay was filled with hundreds of watercraft.

*Variety* took a slightly different stance. Recent quotes of $1.5 million to get the park moving "must have gone for ground purchase. Certainly the equipment does not show it." Claiming the park was "half-finished," it cited stacks of lumber stored throughout the park, unimpressive buildings and an entrance arch described as "unimposing." Added to its list were inferior chairs in the dance hall. It lauded the centerpiece circle swing and the free acts, particularly the Flying Banvards, a high-flying trapeze group that had performed for the Ringling Brothers Circus. Though the skating rink was open, the roof was still under construction, and building material was scattered about. The magazine's final barb came at the expense of the patrons themselves being described as "rather rough" and akin to the class of citizenry that frequented the Fort George amusement area in northern Manhattan.

*Billboard* was much more favorable. While acknowledging the unavailability of some attractions, it was reported that there was plenty to do for the "enormous" crowd. The "fine" roller rink and dance hall were working at capacity into the evening. The lengthy fireworks display in the evening was described as "unusually excellent." Kudos were also thrown to Professor

Mignon, leader of the Garden City Band that provided the free bandstand shows. The article also lauded the fact that all attendants looked sharp in their uniforms of a golden hue with white facings, white caps and tan shoes. The article concluded, "The layout at Golden City is excellent. It enjoys a five cent fare from any part of Brooklyn and will be well patronized."

Estimates of the opening day crowd were 30,000, even though train lines reported overcrowded conditions. But as word caught on, the patronage numbers grew enormously. A newspaper account reported an estimated crowd of 150,000 on June 10, 1907, barely a week after the opening. In that same account, booming business was reported for *Robinson Crusoe*, "Love's Journey," the Flying Lady and Wormwood's bear and dog circus. Another thrill ride dubbed the "Double Whirl" was gaining in popularity. It was essentially a combination of a merry-go-round and small Ferris wheels. A series of wheels, each holding six couples, was suspended from the merry-go-round. Each wheel revolved quickly as the merry-go-round went in its circle.

Filling out the first year's attractions were the Balletzar Sisters from Germany, a gymnastics sextet, Freeman the handcuff expert, sharpshooter "Miss Sunbeam," gymnasts Silvern and Emerie and the Barlows' breakaway ladder act. Dida amazed audiences with his feats of illusion, one of which was to make a beautiful woman appear and then disappear before their very eyes. As an innovation, daily changes of circus acts occurred throughout the season to entice return visitors.

The first season did not run without glitches. In addition to the aforementioned overcrowded trains and the delayed openings of the park and several major attractions, other events created challenges. A power failure in August 1907 created havoc one evening. The sporadic outages caused intermittent flashing and flickering of the countless lights in the park. It was reported that some in attendance thought it was part of a light show as they shrieked with delight. Others were not amused and were inconvenienced, if not frightened, when their electric cars were stalled at the apex of their rides or in dark tunnels. On another August night, during the fireworks display, a young child was injured when an errant unexploded mortar struck her in the head.

Just before those occurrences, total control of Golden City Park was transferred to Warner's Canarsie Amusement Company from the Golden City Construction Company. It is believed that the construction company was initially formed by the Traver Circle Swing Company. Warner's company, with the backing of several well-heeled "Brooklyn capitalists" (per a newspaper description), was a regularly incorporated company

Golden City's piers jut out into the harbor. The pier on the left was the dance hall. Its twin to the right was the skating rink. *Courtesy of Bob Stonehill.*

formed for the express purpose of further developing and operating Golden City Park. Immediately, Warner announced plans for expansion and improvements for the following season. Warner foresaw a park that would grow from nine acres to around fifty acres over time. He boasted that he would build new attractions that would surpass in excellence any to be found in rival amusement parks. The great expansion of the amusement area never took place.

The ink on the transfer contracts barely had time to dry before the new management was confronted with labor strife. Some employees were let go, and others were reassigned to other jobs in the park. The dismissed employees were "drawing fancy salaries and doing very little to earn them," according to Mr. Warner, and he referred to them as "trouble makers." In addition, all workers were owed nine days' pay from before the changeover. Mr. Warner countered that he had offered the workers the back pay, but they refused to accept it because he would not promise to return them to their positions in the park.

The workers consulted with the Legal Aid Society to determine if they had a matter for legal proceedings. The claimants also felt that they were working under a season's contract. The strife caused operational problems in the park. Striking workers included acrobats and attraction actors. As negotiations continued over the back pay issue, many workers refused to work, and several attractions were curtailed as a result. Eventually, the dispute was resolved.

The rest of the season finished uneventfully, and most considered the opening year a huge success. Even the perimeter businesses outside the park's gates and walls reported strong sales. Hotels, restaurants, Japanese ballgames, the boating concerns and a variety of other concessions benefited from the throngs visiting Golden City.

The second season brought about some additions and changes as promised. In addition to new acts and expanded amusements, a one-price admission for attractions was instituted. That fee entitled the visitor admission to twenty-five of the park's attractions. The one-price admission cost was twenty-five cents.

William J. Warner Jr. began the park's advertising campaign well before the second season's opening day. Again, the ads emphasized a "five-cent fare from New York and Brooklyn" and the claim that Golden City was reachable by all elevated and trolley lines. The season began without the hitches of the previous year, and there were no indications that it was anything but a successful year.

Things would change dramatically in 1909. Amusement park owners always faced many uncertainties and obstacles that could make or break a season. Poor weather on weekends could render a season unprofitable. Competition from newly developed parks could crimp the bottom line. But nothing put fear into owners' lives more than fire. The strike of a match, an errant electrical spark, a discarded cigar or an arsonist's evil intentions with a gasoline can could bring down an entire park within hours. Most parks' major attractions, including the Ferris wheels, roller coasters and carousels, were constructed of wood. Most other concessions and stalls were built of wood frame as well. Firefighters were hampered by many issues but most importantly by lack of water pressure.

All was going well in preparation for opening day of the 1909 season scheduled for May 9. Many improvements in the park had been completed. But on the day before the opening, May 8, 1909, fire struck Golden City Park. A two-story structure that served as a restaurant broke out in flames, possibly as a result of a grease fire. The fire was first noticed by the restaurant's manager, who ran frantically outside shouting, "Fire!"

Volunteers near the site reacted quickly but were no match for the spreading flames and smoke. Valiant firefighters from Engine Company

157 in Canarsie village, under the direction of Battalion Chief Donohue, were the first to respond. Heroically, they formed a human wall between the raging flames and some of the prized amusements as they battled the blaze and desperately tried to check its advance. Despite their best efforts, it was reported that at least half of the park was destroyed in the inferno.

Just outside the park, three hotels (the Golden City Hotel, the Sunset Hotel and Tutze's Hotel) were quickly destroyed. Several witnesses said at least two of the hotels could have been saved if the firefighters' hose had not been crushed under a collapsing portion of the park's arched entrance. Also, as Engine Company 157 was responding, one of its horses stumbled and fell on the railroad tracks. While the engine continued on, the tender carrying the hoses was delayed twenty minutes, allowing the flames a good head start. Other fire companies responded from Brownsville, Flatbush and East New York. Deputy Chief Lally from Brooklyn headquarters helped coordinate the effort.

A large roller coaster was one of several large attractions that was spared. In addition, "Love's Journey," the scenic railway (designed by William Mangels) and several other smaller attractions were saved. The dance hall, restaurant, park office and most of the amusements in the front of the park were destroyed.

Police from local precincts had all they could do to control the crowds from nearby and others from outlying areas who were attracted to the inferno. The flames were seen from miles away. Owner William J. Warner Jr. rescued some payroll records and several thousand dollars in cash from his office next to the restaurant. Estimates of the damage ranged from $100,000 to $200,000. The only structure with insurance was the restaurant, in the amount of $1,000.

Warner could only watch as his investment was going up in smoke. "I am ruined. All the money I have in the world is invested in this park," he lamented. But after some reflection, plans were made to somehow open the park the next day, its scheduled opening. The skating rink would be converted to the dance hall. Repairs would take a week or so to get the large roller coaster back in operation. Burned debris would be cleared out of sight. It is not known if, in fact, the park opened on schedule. Attractions were repaired, and new ones came about over the next several years.

Several beautifully crafted carousels graced the grounds over the years at Golden City, but it was "Murphy's" carousel that arguably was the favorite. In 1912, master carvers Solomon Stein and Harry Goldstein created the carousel that would entertain tens of thousands throughout the rest of the

# BROOKLYN

A carousel built by Solomon Stein and Harry Goldstein for Golden City was housed in this building. It was owned and operated by Murphy and Nunley. The building and carousel were later transported to Baldwin, New York. *Courtesy of Cradle of Aviation Museum/Nunley's Carousel.*

park's tenure. The pair's Artistic Carousel Company was located on nearby Gates Avenue. Their carousels were widely known for outstanding design, workmanship and artistry. The carousel was owned and operated by Timothy Murphy and William Nunley, partners in the Merley Corporation, operators of numerous carousels in the Northeast. The carousel is still operating, as will be discussed later.

On July 17, 1915, a fierce electrical storm tore through Canarsie, and it did not spare Golden City. The major damage was done to the giant roller coaster, which was considered a total loss by concessionaire Louis Bernt. Several other attractions were damaged as well.

The Warner Amusement Company continued to run Golden City Park until Irving and Jacob "Jack" Rosenthal came along. The brothers immigrated with their large family to New York from Russia in 1902. As a child, Irving sold newspapers on the Lower East Side to help with the family's support. While still youngsters, they sold souvenir pails and shovels on the beach at Coney Island and managed to save $15,000. They then purchased a secondhand carousel that operated in an amusement park in Connecticut. They parlayed the profit from that venture and found their way to Golden City. Later, the pair would own and operate the famous Cyclone at Coney Island in its first year (1927). Perhaps they are most remembered, though, for purchasing and operating Palisades Amusement Park starting in 1934. They ran that historic park through its glory years until 1971, when the land was sold to developers.

Their saga at Golden City began when Irving and Jack were still very young men. In 1919, they began operating several concessions at Golden City. By opening day 1921, the entire park was under the management of the Rosenthal brothers. The park had been run down a bit in the preceding few years, but the Rosenthals rejuvenated it. The park thrived under the brothers' management. The Rosenthals scheduled many special events during the park's seasons to attract even more visitors. In August 1921, they contracted with L.M. Rich to promote "baby shows" at the park. The weeklong contest culminated with a coronation of the "queen" and "king" babies. The turnouts were huge. Other promotions included free "kiddie days," prizes for the mothers of the largest families, baby carriage decoration contests and public weddings. A 1921 *Billboard* article described the Rosenthals: "Watch this shore under their [Rosenthals'] management…they are going to startle the amusement park world in the not very distant future."

Concessions and attractions evolved over time. It is a good guess that the big theater productions were becoming passé. Folks were looking more for thrill and amusement rides. Bumper cars built by the Dodgem Company made an appearance in 1921. The park was renovated end to end for the 1922 season. Rides operating in 1922 included several coasters, the Whip, the Frolic, an aeroplane swing, the aforementioned bumper cars, a mammoth new fun house, a refurbished Old Mill, a yacht race, the Kentucky Derby (a popular group participation game), pony tracks, numerous shooting galleries, Venetian swings, the Japanese Rolldown, a new chutes ride and the Balloon Racer, among many others.

An Indian Village was also in operation toward the rear of the park around this time. Local residents often witnessed the cowboys and Indians exercising their horses on the local streets of Canarsie in the early morning hours. By this time, the Borough Rapid Transit Railroad alone was reporting fifty to seventy thousand patrons every Sunday using the train to attend Golden City. This does not take into account others who approached the park by other means of transportation.

In July 1924, another huge blaze erupted just outside the park, destroying a dozen buildings and one hundred boats along the waterfront, but this time the park was spared. The Rosenthals' Golden City Arena was constructed just outside the amusement area around 1924. The brothers promoted boxing matches that became wildly popular. Both amateurs and professionals plied their skills in the outdoor arena. The amateur bouts and competitions were considered precursors to the famous Golden Gloves tournaments held by the *New York Daily News* starting in 1927. The Rosenthals' Golden City Arena was so successful around this time that they felt they were making more profit from it than from the amusements.

In February 1927, the Rosenthal Brothers Amusement Company extended its tenure by signing a twenty-one-year lease to operate Golden City at a total cost of $2 million. The brothers planned to invest another $500,000 in improvements after the city built a new steel pier out in the bay. The new pier was four hundred feet wide and six hundred feet long. Docking privileges would bring even more revenue to Golden City's coffers. Among other improvements were two new entrances to the park strategically planned to meet arriving patrons who traveled by train or ferry. The Municipal Ferry ran from the Rockaways to the newly installed pier at Canarsie.

Inside the park, a saltwater pool measuring two hundred feet in both length and width would be ready for the opening of the 1927 season. Two new midways were being built over the winter, and a new steel roller coaster was being planned. By 1930, other rides had been added, including a Caterpillar ride and another electric scooter attraction. The Gold Mine took "prospectors" on a tunnel ride as they sat in miniature mining cars. Daredevil acts like the Metro-Brothers' "Wall of Death" added to the park's allure. In this attraction, motorcyclists climbed nearly perpendicular circular walls at high rates of speed.

On a bitter cold morning on January 28, 1934, the scourge of fire again visited Golden City. The inferno, described as the fire district's worst in twenty-six years, dealt a knockout, if not fatal, blow to the amusement park. Numerous local establishments and homes were also victims of the blaze. After the fires were extinguished, the scenic railway eerily kept its outline in a charred state. The Golden City Park Arena was consumed by the flames. Many other concessions were destroyed.

Later in 1934, the Golden City Amusement Park Company's president was Milton Sheen. Sheen was a Brooklyn lawyer. His clients included Golden City's Rosenthal brothers, who walked away from Canarsie when the future looked bleak. With virtually no experience in amusement parks, Sheen somehow managed to make the park marginally profitable again.

Despite this infusion of new energy, the park struggled along for several more years, but its glory days were fast becoming faded memories. Nightly movie revivals brought in respectable crowds by 1938 as Sheen clung to the hope of his park's revival. By this time, the Rosenthal brothers were already creating a new fortune with their Palisades Amusement Park in New Jersey.

Crowds mill around on a busy day at Golden City Park. A Horton's ice cream stand is just to the right of center. It was the most popular ice cream of the era. *Courtesy of Bob Stonehill.*

In the spring of 1938, plans for the Brooklyn-Queens Circumferential highway (later the Belt Parkway) were well underway. Robert Moses and his planners outlined the highway's route and the properties that needed to be bought. Brooklyn Borough president Raymond Ingersoll received approval from the Board of Estimate to purchase the Golden City Park property in addition to other properties. Veiled offers by the Board of Estimate for improvements at Golden City Park and the waterfront area were eventually discarded. The park was doomed in the name of automobile transportation. The first (and only) "annual" bathing beauty contest was held at Golden City on August 18, 1938. The winner was crowned "Miss Canarsie."

On December 5, 1938, steam shovels tore through what was left of Golden City Park and demolished thirty-eight of the remaining buildings. Concessionaires sued by stating that Mr. Moses had agreed to give them more time to close things down properly. Regardless of the suit's outcome, the park's fate was forever sealed.

Virtually no memorabilia remains of Golden City Park. "Murphy's" carousel is a major exception. Seeing the writing on the wall in early 1938, William Nunley moved the carousel and its large framed building to Baldwin, Long Island, before the demolition crews arrived. In 1940, it reopened as Nunley's Carousel and Amusements on Sunrise Highway, where it was the centerpiece of a small but successful amusement area. Nunley's was a local favorite and had a good run until it closed in 1995.

When Nunley's closed, many of its amusements were sold off, and the carousel's fate was in doubt. Its last owners, the Lercari family, were ready to sell the famous carousel at auction, either as individual pieces or as a whole. The sale of individual horses would have meant the end of the carousel as a ride. However, outcries from citizens, public officials (who secured a court injunction), schoolchildren and carousel preservationists spared the cherished carousel. The County of Nassau purchased the iconic carousel, realizing its historic value and what it meant to generations of Long Islanders. Meticulous restoration work was funded by various sources, including Pennies for Ponies, where schoolchildren collected pennies to "adopt" a pony for $2,000.

On Saturday, May 2, 2009, the famed carousel proudly began operating again inside a majestic pavilion along Museum Row in Garden City. Its forty-one wild-eyed horses and one lion are once again creating a new legion of fans while preserving a piece of Golden City Park history as well.

Billy Joel, Long Island's legendary rock star, paid tribute to the carousel when his "Waltz No. 1" piano solo was subtitled "Nunley's Carousel."

# 4
# QUEENS

## NORTH BEACH

Since 1939, LaGuardia Airport has served as a major airline hub in the New York City metropolitan area. Whether strolling along the street of a northern Queens neighborhood or watching a New York Mets home game, one can't help but notice the sights and sounds of the frequent departures and arrivals. The airport separates Bowery Bay from Flushing Bay close to neighborhoods like Astoria, Steinway, Jackson Heights and East Elmhurst. Over one hundred years ago, the area took on a completely different tone. The area was the venue for one of New York City's great seaside resorts and amusement areas for several decades.

William (Wilhelm) Steinway was a hugely successful entrepreneur in northern Queens who became best known as a premier piano manufacturer. He saw the coast along Bowery Bay as an ideal location for a resort area. In the mid-1880s, the waters were considered to be pristine. The bluffs and wooded shoreline created a natural beauty lying only a short distance from Manhattan. Along with a few other investors, Steinway laid out plans for a pleasant summer resort area that would cater to local German American families, including those in Steinway's employ.

He helped form the Bowery Bay Beach Improvement Company in May 1896 to bring his plans to fruition. His chief collaborator in the project was another local, George Ehret, considered to be one of the world's greatest and wealthiest brewers. Ehret foresaw a business opportunity on the horizon as

The dance pavilion on the left was operated by Henry Daufkirk (also spelled "Daufkirch"). He was the unofficial "mayor" of North Beach. To the right of the Ferris wheel is a carousel house.

his renowned beverages would no doubt quench the thirst of the anticipated throngs. It should be noted that by 1891, Bowery Bay Beach was renamed North Beach.

Working with capital of $20,000, the group purchased the necessary properties along Bowery Bay Beach. Landscapers removed and replanted trees. Roads were either added or extended. A sea wall of over 2,000 feet in length was erected along the shoreline. A huge pier (variously reported from 500 feet to 700 feet long and 110 feet wide) was constructed into the bay to accommodate large steamships. The pier would be known as the Grand Pier. An artificial lake called Spring Lake was established. Additional hotels were built to provide for the needs of those visitors who preferred a longer stay as they sought fresh air, rest and enjoyment away from the heat and squalor of Manhattan and the other boroughs. Swimmers could avail themselves of two large bathhouses.

Since the beach area was brilliantly illuminated at night, bathers could enjoy the cooling waters under the stars. Later, as an alternative, a swimming pool was constructed that used the most modern filtration methods. Sailboats, rowboats and other aquatic devices created a busy scene just off the beach.

Several steam-powered carousels were installed. George W. Kremer's Silver Spring carousel (built by Looff) was situated near the Silver Spring swimming pool at Eightieth Street. Its crown was decorated with portraits of the twenty-four presidents, and young and old delighted in riding the camels, horses and large dogs. The "Junction Carrousel," also built by Looff and possibly owned by Kremer, was housed in a brick structure with a fanciful roof. Both Looff carousels sported three-abreast standers and jumpers. A large Ferris wheel, a switchback railroad and a large dance hall added to the variety of activities.

Steinway and Ehret bought the dock front on the East River at East Ninety-ninth Street in 1887. Steamers departed that wharf in Manhattan for the thirty-minute journey to the resort area's Grand Pier at a cost of ten cents. Access to the beach area was also provided by the Astoria Ferry from East Ninety-second Street for a three-cent fare. Upon arrival in Astoria, the cars of the Steinway Electric Company transported the fun-seekers to the recreational area for an additional fee. The resort was also accessible via several Brooklyn ferry lines.

The beer gardens, casinos and hotels fared particularly well in the early years. Sanford's Point Hotel hosted special promotional events and club gatherings, all while serving up George Ehret's beer on tap, of course. Kohler's New Pavilion's specialties were its sausages and soda water, and it also provided shooting galleries, swings and dancing. Henry Daufkirch's Bay View House was a popular gathering spot with live entertainment on the weekends. Henry himself was dubbed "the mayor of North Beach" for his convivial nature. When Prohibition helped put an end to the glory years of North Beach, Daufkirch transferred his energies to Schuetzen Park in Astoria. He died in 1942. Some establishments such as the Club House and Grand Pavilion catered to finer tastes with their distinctive liquors and cigars. Meals could be ordered at any hour, and they were cooked to order.

In 1888, the popular "chutes" was added. Claims were made that it was the largest chutes in the world. The ramp was built at a thirty-one-degree incline and was measured at three hundred feet in length. The passenger boats could attain speeds upward of an incredible seventy-two miles per hour. Roller coasters would not attain that velocity for many decades.

By 1890, electric trolleys had begun running to the park. After William Steinway passed away in 1896, things began to change. The Bowery Bay Beach Improvement Company was restructured. The focus shifted to more amusement rides and attractions. Also around this time, the area was gaining a reputation as a gambling mecca. It was often referred to as the "Monte Carlo of Greater New York." The Seventy-fourth Precinct opened a substation in 1899 at the resort area to monitor the weekend crowds and

The "chutes" was one of the earliest attractions at North Beach. Claimed to be the biggest anywhere, it was a crowd favorite for many years. *Courtesy of Bob Stonehill.*

to control the blatant gambling in public. However, police officers were often encouraged to turn their heads the other way when gambling activities were observed being conducted on privately owned properties. The substation remained open only during the entertainment season.

The entertainment zone soon stretched about three miles along Shore Road. More concert halls, popcorn machines, amusement rides and food stalls populated the once pristine and serene waterfront. Gala Park, a large amusement concession, opened in 1901. By 1903, Sunday crowds rarely numbered fewer than 60,000. There are reports of crowds soaring to 150,000 on holidays and special promotion days. Mid-week charter boats from Long Island and New Jersey helped spread out the numbers more evenly over the course of a week. Bob's Casino, Kohler's Hotel and Pavilion, Bonhag's Pavilion, Fort Andersen, the Terminal Hotel, the Park Theater, Sanford's Point Hotel (serving "only" George Ehret's lager beer on draught) and the Jackson Point Hotel (with its bowling lanes), among others, brought in a dizzying array of singers, musicians, magicians, comedians, dancers, burlesque performers and novelty acts. Some venues stayed open all year long.

There was plenty to amuse young and old. In addition to the chutes, "mammoth" carousels, toboggan slides, pony tracks, a Ferris wheel and a miniature railway were advertised. A Traver circle swing swung riders over the edge of the bay near the Great Pier.

The area clung to only a few vestiges of its rich history. Most interestingly, perhaps, was the abandoned burial grounds high atop a bluff above Bowery Bay. One of its earliest settlers, Daniel Rapelye, built a homestead and raised a family around the start of the eighteenth century. Upon his death, he was placed in the family's burial ground just north of the home. The cemetery would eventually include many members of his ancestry. By 1903, Gala Park was in full swing. Juxtaposed with the barely standing gravestones, a roaring roller coaster and a lively dance hall surrounded the site. Picnickers could be observed eating their lunches amongst the headstones and using the remaining foundation stones from the mansion as tables for their provisions.

By 1904, Gala Park was billing itself as "Nature's Own Playground." It offered a uniqueness that set it apart from most other beach resorts. The ground gently undulated toward the crescent beach, and its clean water was supported by a backdrop of ravines, some of which retained the look and feel of primal forests. Its amusement offerings expanded to include a Simian village, a zip ride and sea lions near the chutes. Most buildings were painted in distinctive bright yellow and blue. The kiosks' domes were serpentine shapes of yellow and black.

The Silver Springs swimming pool was a large draw. It was built in 1901, replacing all or part of Silver Lake. The pool was located near the terminus of the Thirty-fourth Street trolley just off Ehret Avenue. Electric pumps worked tirelessly to force fresh salt water into the pool, where often a thousand or more bathers frolicked at any given time.

An artificial waterfall was added to the chutes. Three toboggan slides operated by the Morris Amusement Company were spread throughout the beach area providing the thrills, screams and roars that are still associated with today's amusement parks. E. Joy Morris, from Philadelphia, also built and operated the "Maple carrousel." It was installed just after the turn of the century.

By 1905, reports indicated that attendance was then averaging between 110,000 and 150,000 on good-weather weekends. Some surmised it was second only to Coney Island in terms of attendance, even surpassing the number of visitors to the Rockaways. No fewer than fifteen concert halls entertained folks into the late hours, and the weekly fireworks displays in the bay were spectacular. It was claimed that North Beach provided more free entertainment than any other New York City beach amusement area.

For the 1906 season, another one of Morris's scenic toboggan slides was added. It was touted to be the highest and longest toboggan ride in the East. Its entrance was a structure of beauty adorned with thousands

This Looff carousel was located near the Silver Spring swimming pool. George Kremer operated the ride. He was the proprietor of many other concessions as well.

of electric lights. A popular novelty act that year was Lockwood, the one-legged cyclist, who dared the running waters of the chutes as he cycled furiously down the ramp. Several of the dance halls underwent renovations with the installation of all-new maple floors. W.J. Wright was the manager of the park at this time.

The following year was a landmark one for North Beach. Announcements were made in January 1907 that another large park concession would be up and running for the start of the season. Stella (Star) Park would be erected at a cost of roughly $1 million. William Seltz, a seltzer water magnate from Brooklyn, acquired the property (and many buildings) to make way for Stella Park. Some of the picturesque boathouses were retained, as was the historic Jackson's Point Hotel. The hotel was overhauled and converted into a first-class establishment.

The new park encompassed 300,000 square feet. Seltz formed the Stella Park Amusement Company and hired L.A. Munger to manage the project. A new electrical plant was installed at a cost of $25,000. The entire park would be brilliantly illuminated in the evening. A grand entrance to the self-contained Stella Park was erected at a cost of $27,000.

The grounds were laid out in picturesque winding paths bordered by lush gardens with several artistic electric fountains as centerpieces. The menu of rides included yet another toboggan ride, another Ferris wheel, a mile-long scenic railway, large and small carousels, several casinos and dance halls. Several bandstands provided free entertainment throughout the day. Restaurants representing the tastes of many nations were scattered about. Special performances of *Electric City by the Sea* illuminated the beach at night. The planned opening day was Memorial Day 1907.

Estimates of projected attendance for the season were astronomical. Stella Park was alternately described as a "fairyland" and a "wonderland" and was being compared to Luna Park and Dreamland at Coney Island, always the barometer for such ventures. Between the new park and Gala Park, it looked as if North Beach was entering its prime years.

Stella Park opened with some special attractions, including *The Fireman's Christmas Eve*, a fire show by Claude L. Hagen. The show played to capacity houses daily and featured a cast of forty entertainers. The Far East show exhibited walled streets and natives from the Orient accompanied by sacred animals. There was a variety show called the *Seven Whirlwinds*. The Radium Theater highlighted the Great LaBlanche in her fire and serpentine dance. Her success led to a long tenure at the park. The *Tidal Wave* became a popular show with its spectacular electrical and scenic effects. The *Arabian Nights* was yet another large production. Illusion shows, a dog and monkey show, dromedary rides, pony rides and electric boat rides in the bay all created a versatile menu of activities.

Skaters enjoyed the huge rink (150 by 60 feet) and the accompanying live music initially provided by the Carrado Band. The sounds of the carousels rang out around North Beach. An older Looff carousel was also operated by Fred Droge. Originally, it featured stationary figures, but when William Mangels rebuilt it, the horses were converted to "jumpers." The Old Mill was always packed. As the season wore on, a sign was posted strategically over the park's front entrance: "Notice! Stella Park is not as yet completed, and never will be, as the management will improve it annually."

Gala Park, perhaps gearing up for its new competition, opened the 1907 season with improvements. Many additional lights were added to its property along the beach. Landscapers installed new hedges, potted plants and numerous new flower beds. Fresh coats of paint adorned the structures. Improvements were made in the chutes and its boats. Several new attractions also debuted. A new featured performer was Ajax in his "Slide for Life." Ajax was suspended from an overhead wire tethered to his teeth as he slid

Stella Park and Gala Park were, by far, the two largest concessions at North Beach. This advertisement promotes the brave bull-fighting feats of Shad Link, a Stella Park favorite.

from the top of the chutes tower into the lake below. Not to be outdone, Dareing, the Handcuff King, escaped from a sack in which he had been sewn. Before being encased, he was bound and gagged—all of this before being tossed into the chutes lake. Anxious onlookers watched in near horror as air bubbles rose to the surface. They implored the handlers to rescue the surely doomed man. But just before the rescue effort was launched, Dareing always managed to bolt to the surface in the nick of time, gasping for breath, much to the crowd's relief and enjoyment.

Another novelty act, Shad Link, the "bull fighter," attracted large crowds on a twice-daily basis starting in the 1907 season. Shad Link, a champion wrestler of some note, claimed that he could wrestle and throw any ferocious bull brought to the arena at Stella Park. Shad had his own stock of bulls as well, but the park's management put out an offer to anyone who wished to bring his own bull to the park for Shad's wrestling pleasure. If Shad could not "throw" the visiting bull, a $500 prize would be awarded to its owner.

Shad, adorned in his customary gray robe, stalked into the "woods" to retrieve his opponent as the crowd anxiously stood by. A black Spanish bull was his victim for matinees, and a big red bull wrestled with him during special evening performances. Link would dance around the bull and taunt it until the time was perfect to grab the beast by the horns and heave it over. Several challenges were made, but it is not known if Shad was successful or if the park doled out any prize money. His act remained popular for a number of years.

Attendance was up dramatically during the season, thanks largely to the heavy advertising by the Stella Park and Gala Park owners. They controlled not only the two large parks but also myriad concessions scattered along the boardwalk, Bowery Bay Road and Maple Avenue. The small concessions included the usual popcorn and peanut stands, cane-rack booths, shooting galleries and smaller music halls. Novelty promotions added throngs. Between July 28 and August 8 in that year, recorded features included a nail-driving contest for women, a shoe-tying contest for boys, a grand baby show (with 1,500 babies entered), a potato-peeling match for ladies and a "battle royal" for boys.

By mid-season, Stella Park's manager L.A. Munger was already announcing plans for the following year. The grounds would be enlarged. New rides would be added, along with more free attractions. Plans included building another large pier to provide space for balloon rides. An upgraded power plant would not only provide more candle power to the park's lighting, but also plans were in place for an electric tower that would be visible for miles around at night. The tower, adorned with hundreds of incandescent bulbs, would be crowned with a blazing star symbolic of the park's name. The total effect was to make Stella Park "one of the best lighted parks in the country."

Yet another scenic railway would encircle the park. It would possess, according to the owners, "dips as death defying as any in greater New York." Boasts were made that visitors returning the following season would barely recognize the resort. The popular Indian Village, under Chief White Deer, would continue its run. The Helter Skelter, Bottomless Well and the Crazy House were free attractions.

A good argument could be made that North Beach had entered its "golden years" at this point. Both Gala and Stella Parks' attractions were modern and popular. The grounds were in pristine condition, and attendance figures were eye-popping. Even along the fringes of the two big parks, North Beach's attractions and concessions thrived. The Cupid Coaster along Bowery Bay drew large crowds. Its riders were showered with a spray of confetti to top off their journeys.

# Lost Amusement Parks of New York City

One of North Beach's many scenic railways can be seen in the background in this photograph. This is the intersection of Grand Boulevard (left) and Crescent Avenue (right). *Courtesy of Bob Stonehill.*

But lurking in the shadows were some ominous signs. The resort area was still drawing a large gambling population. While women and children enjoyed the beach, rides and attractions, many men preferred the action at the casinos, hotels and alleys. While the beer gardens and the hotel bars prospered, drunkenness was a common state of affairs. Additionally, there were reports that the bay area water was not as clear and pollution free as it had been. This insidious condition raised concerns about the impact it might have in the near future.

The opening of the 1908 season saw George W. Tomasso as the operating manager of Stella Park. Munger was still running the day-to-day business of Gala Park. Ownership in both parks remained the same. Firework shows were still held on Thursday nights.

It wouldn't be until the 1909 season that fireworks' displays were expanded to two nights (Tuesdays and Thursdays). Stella Park opened the new season with a new Wild West Show. One of the new free circus acts was the "One-Armed Boy Wonder," who performed two acts daily of daring high-wire acrobatics. Carousels operated by George W. Kremer and Fred Droge continued to please one and all. The annual grand five-day carnival in September capped off another successful season at North Beach. It was described as one of the most "pretentious" in local history and one of the biggest events up to that point at North Beach. A huge parade with floats and the crowning of the festival's queen started things off. The carnival concluded with a fifty-five-minute fireworks display that was witnessed by

> **---FOR RENT---**
> **Stella Park, North Beach, N. Y.**
> An up-to-date Amusement Park to lease upon very advantageous terms or percentage. Lessee have entire control of Park and 13 large buildings fully equipped—Fire and Flame building, Knights of Arabia Theatre, Devil's Theatre, Shooting Gallery, Johnstown Flood Theatre, Skating Rink, Fortune Teller, Ice Cream Parlor, Russian Building, Japanese Stand, Carousel, Restaurant, Etc.
> ACCESSIBLE FROM ALL PARTS OF NEW YORK. Street railway stops at the Main Entrance. The park is well lighted by our own Electric Power House.
> **For Information, apply to THEO. BLAU, North Beach, L. I., N. Y.**

This 1911 *Billboard* advertisement by Stella Park's owner William Seltz may have been triggered by warning signs that would prove detrimental to future business.

over fifty thousand people. Among the show's highlights were an American flag that burned red, white and blue for a full ten minutes and a miniature Niagara Falls of fire that lasted an equal amount of time.

In subsequent years, however, it appeared that few new rides, if any, were added. The carousels, James Thom's Ferris wheel and Morris's toboggan slides were still popular. Live acts were rotated to keep the entertainment fresh (and at lower cost than adding rides). The Benedettos became a popular comedic aerial high ladder act in 1910 at Gala Park. Many new shows were added to entertain young ones, including Mr. and Mrs. Monk's Monkey Show. Moving picture shows were updated weekly.

On March 14, 1911, a *Billboard* advertisement listed Stella Park "for rent." The lessees would have total control of the thirteen buildings and all of the attractions. It is unclear why Mr. Seltz opted for this plan. Attendance was still strong, even though it appeared some of the attractions were becoming a little worn. But he might have been heeding some of the aforementioned warning signs.

Landscapers and painters provided a general sprucing up of North Beach before the opening of the 1912 season. But aside from these cosmetic improvements, little seemed to be added in the way of new attractions. In a cost-cutting measure, it was announced that firework displays would once again be reduced from two nights per week to one. The year got off to an ominous start in another way. On opening day, a fire broke out in the Old Mill along the beach. The quick thinking of its manager prevented a possible greater disaster. Upon seeing the fire, and after notifying the municipal fire brigade, he immediately had a hose line run from the chutes pond, and by

The "onion skin"–styled roof in front of the Ferris wheel was a common feature at Gala Park. Note the pony track concession in the foreground.

utilizing the powerhouse's pump, he was able to douse the flames. The Old Mill and Joe's Restaurant were total losses.

Around this time, Gala Park was still considered the emerald gem of North Beach with its sprawling, manicured lawns and its bounty of blossoming plants and rare foliage. To many, it was a veritable fairyland aside from the noisy and busy rides and attractions. It remained a favored spot for picnickers throughout its run. But there were rumbles of more troubles on the horizon, as the waters became more unappealing and the specter of Prohibition was looking more and more formidable. For a resort lined with beer gardens, casinos and hotels, alcohol played a large part in its ultimate success or failure.

As early as October 1912, at a Board of Estimate meeting, members floated the idea of creating a quiet public park at North Beach to replace the honky-tonk atmosphere of the area. The tawdry tango dance halls and bars built around the periphery of the amusement areas were becoming a public nuisance. In response, Gala Park, under the new management of Sam Abrams, and other concessionaires dug in, made some improvements and readied for the opening of the 1913 season. May 18 saw a record opening day crowd. Some new attractions had been added, including the Giggler at Gala Park. But most of the rides were showing their age.

Stella Park was now leased to a number of Manhattan merchants. Its name was changed to Queen's Park and officially opened on June 14. Its new general managers, Edward Goldberg and Benjamin Hirsch, would oversee the ten-acre park. Free admission remained a standard policy. Once again, firework displays were held twice weekly, on Tuesdays and Thursdays. The swimming pool's business was better than ever, possibly because the bay's water was becoming less attractive. Nearby Rikers Island was being used by the city as a refuse dump, greatly adding to the bay's pollution. The once abundant shellfish harvested in the bay and used by the local restaurants had become inedible.

In early January 1914, a storm ravaged Flushing Bay and North Beach. High winds and high tides combined to destroy the stone sea wall along the shore near Gala Park. Boat basins and several yacht clubs sustained major damage. Still, the 1914 season opened on schedule. The biggest improvement was to the swimming pool. A modern filtration plant was built and was considered to be a model for all future plants. New amusements included "The House that Jack Built" (in which the rooms were built at odd angles and levels) and the "Hindu Stand," described as a "freak laughter provoking creation from the Orient."

On Decoration Day 1916, North Beach opened the season with a giant firework show and a mammoth parade featuring a band of almost two hundred men. The only new attraction announced was "Along the Nile," which housed sixty-five alligators. The exhibit was intended to be both entertaining and educational. Sam Abrams entered his third year as Gala Park's manager.

In early September 1916, another fire resulted in the destruction of the recently remodeled Unter Der Linden, a popular two-story resort building located on a 130- by 100-foot plot between Ehhret and Broad Avenues. Several nearby structures were damaged as well, including one of Morris's scenic railways along Ehret Avenue. Were it not for the quick thinking of a train conductor, the situation might have been much worse. Still other negative events were having an impact on North Beach.

In February 1917, the long-standing North Beach Amusement Company (formerly the Bowery Bay Beach Improvement Company) announced its intentions of suspending its activities at North Beach. It cited business losses attributable to an infantile paralysis epidemic, which restricted swimming at the beach as ordered by the Board of Health. In addition, several fires had brought about the losses of several buildings, including a dance hall. In its place, the North Beach Leasing Corporation began leasing property at the resort in order to reduce its operations. Among its officers were George Kremer and E. Joy Morris, two longtime proprietors at North Beach. While some concessions opened for the 1917 season, many did not. With the beach no longer a lure, the handwriting was on the wall. Additionally, World War I was the nation's main concern. With the war creating anti-German sentiment, venerable German owners and operators at North Beach were being looked at differently.

With the passage of the Eighteenth Amendment to the Constitution that banned alcohol in January 1919, North Beach, like many other resorts and establishments, could not absorb this crippling blow. The amusement area clung to life for several more seasons. The big pier was no longer usable, and it sadly burned in a spectacular fire caused by an electrical problem in October 1925. Trolley lines were closing down.

The last remaining roller coaster made its final run in 1925. By 1926, only remnants of scenic railways, concession stands, a carousel shed and a few other amusement rides existed. Tall weeds had overtaken the once beautiful picnic area. Gala Park had been reduced to a weeded woodland enclosed by weather-beaten walls. Its high-arched entrance still stood, but the lettering "Gala Park" was barely discernible. A few concessions, including refreshment stands, a few shooting galleries and games, struggled to survive as weekend visitors, now largely Greek families, provided some support. A few of the remaining hotels reverted to family residences.

Koehler's Dance Pavilion, owned by George Kremer, burned to the ground on April 21, 1927. Kremer had used the building to store amusement devices he operated at the resort for many years. Among the items lost in the blaze were a carousel and numerous coaster cars. Perhaps the final chapter in North Beach's amusement era occurred on January 24, 1928, when gale-force winds blew down a good portion of the abandoned roller coaster once operated by George Anderson. The structure smashed into a nearby home. Fortunately, no one was injured.

Rumors abounded about the future of the former resort area. Housing developers showed an interest. The City of New York was considering park construction. But a surprise twist came in the form of a 105-acre private flying field named the Glenn H. Curtiss Airport (renamed shortly after as the North Beach Airport) that opened on June 15, 1929. Roughly 103 acres along the waterfront were held in abeyance for a projected park. The park never came to fruition. Instead, the land was graded, and remnants of the amusement area were buried.

At Mayor Fiorello LaGuardia's urging, the City of New York decided to build a commercial airport within city limits encompassing a vast tract of land, forever sealing the fate of the once-thriving area of North Beach. With the backing of the federal Works Progress Administration, construction began in 1937. LaGuardia Airport was dedicated on October 15, 1939.

## Rockaways' Playland

Over time, the Rockaway peninsula in Queens, New York, had numerous large amusement concessions. The focus of this section is Rockaways' Playland, the longest-running amusement park in the history of the Rockaways. Rockaways' Playland was located on the Rockaway peninsula between Rockaway Beach Boulevard and the beach from Beach Ninety-eighth Street to Beach Ninety-seventh Street. The original property was bought by L.A. Thompson in 1901 adjacent to the property George C. Tilyou bought in 1900. Tilyou's parcel in Rockaway became Steeplechase Park.

Tilyou was a well-known name in the entertainment field. He is probably most noted for his role in making Coney Island one of the most famous amusement parks in the world. At Rockaways' Steeplechase, Tilyou installed rides he had purchased from the 1900 Pan-American Exposition in Buffalo, New York. One ride was the famous steeplechase, where riders rode horses around a track. He also built a two-story bathhouse one thousand feet long. The bathhouse was fronted by a boardwalk.

Thompson was best known for his work with roller coasters. Many people refer to Thompson as the "father of the modern coaster." By the time of his death, he held thirty patents relating to roller coasters. Thompson's company, L.A. Thompson Scenic Rail Company, built fifty coasters in the United States during its existence. His scenic railroads were often built to look like mountains with a series of tunnels cut into them.

Thompson's Amusement Park originally consisted of a fun house, shooting gallery and a skee-ball ramp when it opened it 1901. Thompson built his midway directly behind Tilyou's bathhouse.

Almost immediately after Steeplechase and Thompson's Park were opened, a dock was built at Beach 98$^{th}$ Street. This dock increased attendance numbers dramatically because visitors could enter either amusement park

Many people came to Rockaways' Playland by steamer. This 1903 photograph shows Old Dominion Line's steamer *Mobjack* at the pier in Rockaway Beach. *Library of Congress.*

directly from the dock instead of having to make their way from the dock at Beach 103rd Street.

The first roller coaster at Thompson's Park was the Gravity Wonder built in 1924. This coaster had an initial drop of seven and a half stories. Locals dubbed the coaster "the hurricane." Located on Beach Ninety-seventh Street, the coaster ran from Howley's Hotel to the beach. When Shore Front Parkway was constructed around 1939, a small part of Playland was condemned. As a result, the roller coaster was shortened.

Thompson died in 1919, and his family continued to run the park until 1927, when a syndicate headed by Robert Katlin bought Thompson's Park for $750,000. The new owners spent $350,000 on the construction of a new arena (which could hold four thousand people), a gymnasium, an Olympic-size swimming pool and new amusements.

May 30, 1928, marked the grand opening of Rockaways' Playland. The park was under the ownership and direction of A. Joseph Geist. Geist, who was born in New York in 1886, held a bachelor's degree from City College and a law degree from New York Law School. In addition to his law practice, he became interested in the entertainment business. Under his direction, Playland became a world-class amusement park. Geist believed three major factors were essential for running the park: safety, cleanliness and beauty.

Olympic tryouts for female swimmers from around the world were held in the new pool on June 30 and July 1, 1928. Every Friday night, the arena was a venue for boxing matches. During the rest of the week, the arena was used for circus performances.

In the summer of 1929, Sunday services were held in the Playland arena. On July 7, 1929, the guest speaker was Wilfred Penny, an eleven-year-old evangelist. Penny was a member of the Church of the Atonement in Brooklyn. He also founded the David Mission of Brooklyn, a missionary society for boys. Penny had previously spoken in Times Square, Brooklyn and at his church.

Major changes to Playland resulted when the arena was torn down in 1930. Noah's Ark was moved to the side, enabling one to look straight down the midway to the beach and the ocean beyond it. Noah's Ark was a walk-through attraction that was shaped like a boat. The boat rested on what was

George C. Tilyou built his Rockaways' Steeplechase in 1900. This Library of Congress photograph is taken at the beach entrance to the park. *Library of Congress.*

designed to look like Mount Ararat in Turkey. As visitors traveled through the ark, they heard the sounds of rain, thunder and Noah giving orders. During all this, the boat rocked gently from side to side, creating the illusion that visitors were on a real boat.

New rides around this time included the Rig-a-Jig, Leaping Lena (an automobile ride in which the cars bounced up and down), Cave O'Laffs and the Pretzel. The Caterpillar, an old standby, was given a major facelift.

By 1936, Rockaways' Playland was advertising that it had twenty-four individual rides and amusements in addition to the largest crystal-clear saltwater pool in the Rockaways. In 1943, Geist added two free aerial acts a day to entertain his customers. He believed you needed to give the people the best possible entertainment, especially when it was free, to keep people coming to the park.

In 1949, Playland underwent its most extensive facelift ever. Joytown, a kiddie park, was added on the Jamaica Bay side. This park featured a merry-go-round for the low price of three cents per ride. A miniature railroad, a pony ride, an airplane ride, auto rides, a Whip and a boat ride were also featured. The kiddie rides were eight cents for children and ten cents for adults. Classic tunes and popular music of the time were played over the loudspeakers.

Many people journeyed to Playland by boats operated by the Wilson Line. These boats traveled from Jersey City, New Jersey, and lower Manhattan. On occasion, boats from Yonkers arrived at the pier opposite Playland. By 1950, efforts were being made to start boat service from Sheepshead Bay as well. This service would make the park more accessible to residents from a wider area of Brooklyn.

Widespread improvements came to Playland again in 1950. Two new adult rides and ten new kiddie rides were installed. The lighting system was modernized to include, for the first time in the Rockaways, 250 eight-foot waterproof fluorescent lights. Searchlights were placed on towers, some with colored lenses, to illuminate the park. One million electric bulbs lit up the buildings and grounds. Meanwhile, the Chamber of Commerce of the Rockaways instituted weekly fireworks displays on Wednesday nights throughout the season.

The hit movie *This Is Cinerama*, produced in 1952, put Rockaways' Playland on the nation's map. When it premiered at the Broadway Theatre in New York, it was front-page news in the *New York Times*. After a black-and-white introduction by Lowell Thomas, a veteran radio announcer, the screen expanded to the full Cinerama screen, and viewers were treated to a series of vignettes. The first vignette in the movie was a ride on Playland's roller coaster, the Atom Smasher. The coaster was designed by Vernon Keenan, a renowned designer of amusement rides, and built by the National Amusement Device Company in 1938.

Cinerama was a movie innovation that started in the 1950s. Movies were filmed using three synchronized cameras sharing a single shutter. They were then shown in theaters on specially built screens made up of a series of hundreds of vertical strips angled to face the audience producing a deeply curved screen. Unlike regular movies, which used one projector, Cinerama movies were shown by simultaneously projecting the images from three 35mm projectors onto the screens. Surround sound was part of the experience so that viewers not only felt the action but also experienced the sound of it. This process had the effect of bringing the viewers into the action so that they felt as though they were actually riding the roller coaster and not simply watching it. The film was immensely popular, and it brought some needed attention to Playland. In 2002, the Library of Congress, declaring the movie "culturally, historically and aesthetically significant," added it to the National Film Registry.

Six hundred children from orphanages, settlement houses and institutions for handicapped children were treated to a free day at Playland in 1953 by the William E. Sheridan Police Post of the American Legion and A. Joseph Geist and his son Richard, owners of the park. The day started with a boat ride aboard the *Liberty Bell*, owned by the Wilson Line, from Manhattan to the park. Upon arrival, the children had refreshments and got to enjoy all the amusements the park had to offer.

Steamer service from Sheepshead Bay, Brooklyn, was finally started in 1954 by the Rockaway Boat Line. Its steamers left every two hours starting at 10:30 a.m. A round-trip ticket from Sheepshead Bay cost $1.10.

By the summer of 1961, Rockaways' Playland was hosting weekly events. Every Monday evening, there were beauty pageants. Children's contests were held on Saturday afternoons. Appearances by disc jockeys and television stars were staged throughout the season. Playland was once again renovated extensively and new rides and attractions were added. The park was open on Saturdays and Sundays from 11:00 a.m. to 7:00 p.m.

When New York City hosted the World's Fair from 1964 to 1965, people believed the mammoth fair would draw visitors away from the area's amusement parks. The president of Playland, Richard Geist, felt the fair would not affect Rockaway, as he believed people would still be attracted to the sand and the ocean. While attendance may have dipped a bit, Playland's attendance returned to what it had been previously once the fair concluded.

A new boat service from Westchester via the Sound Steamship Line's new boat, the *Bay Belle*, was initiated in 1964. At that time, Playland offered more than sixty-five rides, games and amusements, according to Geist.

By the 1970s, park attendance had begun to decline. Large crowds seemed to arrive only on holidays such as the Fourth of July. People were perhaps finding Playland somewhat worn and obsolete.

Rockaways' Playland was used as a backdrop for the movie *Sophie's Choice* in 1982. Meryl Streep played the main character, Sophie Zawistowski, who was portrayed as living in Brooklyn in 1947. One of the movie's scenes took place in Playland. The park was transformed to appear as it might have in 1947, with the actors and extras dressed in period clothes. One scene shows Nathan, Sophie's boyfriend, lifting her out of the Calypso ride in the park. Streep won the Academy Award for Best Actress for her role in the movie.

When Rockaways' Playland closed for the season in 1985, the owner had reason to believe it would reopen the following year. But a steep increase in liability insurance, the changing tastes of visitors and the fact that the Rockaways were declining as a summer resort forced the owner to keep the gates closed. Late in 1986, the property was sold to developers who planned to build a $30 million condominium complex on the site.

Today, nothing remains of the once vibrant park that entertained millions of people during its eighty-six-year run.

# 5
# BRONX

## STARLIGHT PARK

Starlight Park and its amusements spanned about two decades, wedged between two of the fiercest wars in American history. The park provided a safety valve of escape for millions before and during the Great Depression era as well. The variety of entertainment ranged from the mere recreational to the classical. From roller coasters, swimming pools, fireworks and sporting events to classical opera and symphony music, Starlight Park offered something for everyone. In operation from 1918 until around 1932 (although the pool, athletic fields and coliseum would linger for many more years), Starlight Park came about in a more unique way than most amusement parks in the city.

To understand the evolution of Starlight Park, one must look first to the creation and development of the Bronx Exposition Park in the West Farms area of the county. It was the site of the Bronx International Exposition (also referred to as the New York International Exposition of Science, Arts and Industries) starting in 1918. While commemorating the 300th anniversary of the settlement of the borough, its underlying objective was to promote international trade. To do so, it provided a venue for American manufacturers to showcase their advancements for visiting business leaders from all over the world. It also served multiple purposes on the local front. On one hand, it was expected that the exposition would spur real estate development in this once dormant area of the Bronx, with its effects rippling

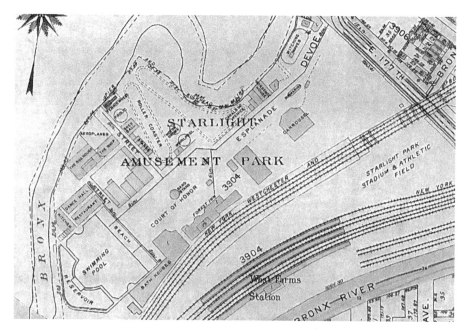

The Bronx River formed a natural border for a good portion of Starlight Park. Note that Starlight Park Stadium was located across the railroad tracks.

up to Westchester County. Along those lines, plans to develop most of the 135-acre William Waldorf Astor estate were already being planned by 1917. Finally, its amusements would provide entertainment, not only for the citizens of the Bronx, but for the other boroughs and outlying areas as well. It was intended to be a permanent fixture on the site.

The park was built on twenty-seven acres of the Astor estate nestled around 177th Street and its natural border, the Bronx River. Its transportation conduit would be the train station at 177th Street at Devoe Avenue, a short ride from midtown Manhattan. In addition, the land was a relative bargain. Harry F. McGarvie, the director-general of the project, took out a twenty-one-year lease on the property. McGarvie had extensive experience in park development, including his work at the Panama-Pacific Exposition of 1914. Groundbreaking ceremonies took place on August 1, 1916. However, no sooner had the shovels broken the soil than McGarvie ran into resistance.

The United States government pulled back some of its support of the project based on its political agenda and the turmoil caused by World War I. It objected to the Latin American–themed buildings. Brazil, in particular, was planning a large exhibition. In addition, since trade with parts of Europe was being restricted, it was felt that the objectives of the exposition were not necessarily in the country's best interest. Fifteen major attractions were designed to stand out among the proposed total of one hundred buildings. Among the planned featured pavilions were the Palace of American Achievements (the largest), the Palace of Fine Arts and the Temple of Liberal Arts. In addition to other American-themed buildings, Spanish and Oriental influences were to be in evidence. Canada planned to open its own pavilion in the exposition's second year. A novel attraction, the Holland Number 9 submarine (the first submarine commissioned by the United States Navy), was transported to the park in May 1917. It became a familiar and curious sight on the grounds until about 1932, when it was reportedly scrapped.

To attract those seeking lighter fare, a giant saltwater swimming pool and bathhouse (built in Spanish Colonial architecture) were constructed. At a reported 350 by 300 feet (the figures vary somewhat), it was touted as the "largest concrete pool in the world." Up to nine thousand bathers could be accommodated. A sand beach (55 by 55 feet) and a wave motion machine created an ocean beach effect. The sand was brought to the park from the Rockaways. Other forms of amusement were either newly constructed or brought to the park from previous locations.

A roller coaster (dubbed a "joy ride through the clouds"), designed by L.A. Thompson, was built on the site. The Ferris wheel built by the Eli Bridge Company of Jacksonville, Illinois, was transported from San Diego, where it had been operating at the Panama-California Exposition. The sixty-foot wheel could spin seventy-two passengers at a time. Each of the twelve cars was named after one of the thirteen original colonies. It is a mystery why one state was not included. Numerous restaurants, picnic areas and live shows rounded out the offerings.

To draw people's attention to the park, a sophisticated lighting system, including revolving searchlights, was designed by General Electric. But by opening day, May 30, 1918, many of the planned exhibits were not to be found. It was evident early on that the amusement portion of the exposition would be its focal point. By the first year's conclusion on November 1, the exposition was deemed a commercial, if not an aesthetic, success.

In its second year, the park began taking on even more of an amusement park motif. *Billboard* advertisements ran by Bronx Expositions, Inc., called the park the "Bronx Exposition and Amusement Park," claiming that it was "the largest and finest pleasure park in America." H.F. McGarvie was the company's president. The park's amusement attractions in that year included

This Eli Bridge Company's Ferris wheel was one of the first amusement attractions brought to Starlight Park. Note that there is a "missing" colony among the cars' names. *From the Optimist, February 1922.*

the Frolic, Witching Waves, the Aeroplane Railway, the Captive Aeroplane, a scenic railway, Venetian Canals, the Whip and two Kentucky Derbies. The Bug House and Nonsense House were added to provide sheer laughs. Rounding out the amusements were Underground Chinatown, Martinka's

Magical Palace, the Tub Race (a jolting and jarring water ride), the U-Boat Dodger and the Whirlpool. A pony track entertained the young ones.

Live entertainment featured the risqué *Shimmyland*, a musical comedy revue. Its proprietor and five performers were the subjects of arrest in July 1919 on charges relating to indecency. Victor's Italian Band, the Zancigs Temple of Mystery and various circus acts rounded out the "flesh acts" (a carnival term for live acts). Of course, the giant roller coaster and grand swimming pool maintained their positions as centerpieces of the amusement area. It is believed that the large Exposition Hall was the only functioning structure held over from the exposition's industrial and cultural plans.

On October 11, 1919, the park officially changed its name to Starlight Park. The board of directors for the Bronx Expositions Corporation invested many thousands of dollars in new rides and amusements for the 1920 season. Early plans included converting Exposition Hall into a dance hall and skating rink. It had become a full-fledged amusement park.

Shortly after opening day in 1920, Starlight Park opened its gates to six thousand children from orphanages around the city. Their benefactor was W.S. Silver, who coordinated the event between the park and automobile dealers from around New York City. The dealers provided the transportation, and the park allowed free admission for the children, ranging in age from six to twelve.

The season saw the addition of scores of smaller concessions, including shooting galleries, myriad games of chance, an "educated" horse and foods of all descriptions. A dark tunnel ride through grottos and other worldly sights named the Hereafter became a popular attraction. The Hereafter was described as presenting "illusions of surpassing beauty based on poetic descriptions of the paths we tread after leaving this earthly place." It was destroyed in a 1924 fire. Admission to the park at this time was fifteen cents.

As the 1920 season came to an end, the park once again hosted a large children's outing. The License Bureau of New York City sponsored a day in the park for eleven thousand youngsters just before the start of the school season. By the time the festivities concluded, it was estimated that the children had consumed 1,500 watermelons, forty barrels of apples, seven thousand quarts of milk and a huge quantity of soda.

However, the end of the amusement season brought no relief to Harry McGarvie, who was also president of the Bronx Expositions Corporation. A breach of contract suit in the amount of $5 million was filed against the corporation by the Exposition Catering Company in December. The suit was one of the largest ever recorded in the entertainment industry.

The suit alleged that the Bronx Expositions Corporation failed to honor its agreement with Exposition Catering in a contract signed on June 9, 1917. The plaintiffs argued that the owners had agreed to build a convention center and a beautiful entrance to the grounds similar to the ones constructed at the St. Louis and Chicago World's Fairs. In addition, the Bronx Expositions Corporation had promised to continue a permanent industrial exposition on the site. Instead, they argued, the defendants had mismanaged their money and built "a cheap amusement park." The Bronx Catering Company claimed it fulfilled its portion of the agreement when it contributed a sum of $200,000 for the contracted improvements. All of that money was "lost," according to the claim. The result of the suit is unknown, but it should be mentioned that Harry McGarvie passed away on April 23, 1922. Additionally, other matters of litigation were piling up as a result of injuries sustained at the park.

This poser (1921) was believed to have been a Broadway chorus girl named Eleanor Tierney. She reportedly married a banker and moved to Larchmont.

A brand-new baseball field was one of the new additions for 1921. Local semiprofessional teams competed throughout the season and would do so for many years. Vaudeville acts had been expanded over the previous years. The open-air stage featured funnyman Marvelous Melville; Miss Velda, an aerial trapeze artist; and the Florence Duo, comedic acrobats. Saxi Holtsworth's Band of Harmony Hounds performed their popular act in the pavilion. An innovative feature called "Fame and Fortune" drew crowds. Folks were filmed, and they were able to see themselves on a screen. Of course, the pool opened on Memorial Day. Helen Sube performed her spectacular high-dive act several times a day at the pool.

A youngster back in this era could enroll in the "Kiddie

One of Paradise Park's roller coasters is shown on the left in this early morning depiction at Amsterdam Avenue, around 193rd Street. Paradise Park was the largest concession at the Fort George amusement area. *Courtesy of Jason Minter.*

It was a steep climb up the stairs to get to John Schultheis's Fort George Hotel and Casino. It was more easily accessible along Audubon Avenue.

The Paradise Park Music Hall (left center) was one of the many venues that featured fine vaudeville acts at Fort George. *Courtesy of Bob Stonehill.*

Riders enjoy the Philadelphia Toboggan Company's #15 carousel at the Palisades Center Mall in West Nyack, New York, in 1999. It survived the devastating fire at Fort George in 1913.

*Above*: The Fort George amusement area is seen at its peak in this circa 1907 postcard. Some rides utilized the cliff's natural terrain. *Courtesy of Bob Stonehill.*

*Right*: There were at least three Ferris wheels on the grounds of Fort George. This one at Paradise Park was believed to be the smallest. *Courtesy of Bob Stonehill.*

This is the boardwalk entrance to Happyland Park. Note the stand on the left selling Horton's Ice Cream. J.M. Horton was the oldest ice cream company in America, dating from 1870. *Courtesy of Bob Stonehill.*

In the background is one of L.A. Thompson's scenic railways designed to look like a mountain with many tunnels built into it at Happyland. *Courtesy of Bob Stonehill.*

Chutes were popular attractions at most amusement parks, including this one at South Beach.

One of the roller coasters that operated at Midland Beach is pictured here. *Courtesy of Bob Stonehill.*

A typical day at Midland Beach, circa 1900, features the bandstand in the center of the scene. *Courtesy of Bob Stonehill.*

The Midland Beach Hotel can be seen on the left side of this postcard. *Courtesy of Bob Stonehill.*

The view from this Ferris wheel at Midland Beach offered passengers a broad vista. *Courtesy of Norman Anderson.*

As the construction of Golden City Park continued, this circa 1906 postcard announced the impending opening of the "New Coney Island" in Canarsie. *Courtesy of Bob Stonehill.*

Signs on either side of the main entrance to Golden City Park announced the special events of the day. *Courtesy of Bob Stonehill.*

Shown as it appears today, "Nunley's" carousel was known as "Murphy's" carousel when it made its debut at Golden City Park. *Courtesy of Cradle of Aviation Museum/Nunley's Carousel.*

Playland was built originally in 1929 on the property that once housed Thompson's Park. *Courtesy of Bob Stonehill.*

The pool at Rockaways' Playland was built in 1929. It was often used for Olympic swimming tryouts. *Courtesy of Bob Stonehill.*

Playland's midway ran for one city block between Beach Ninety-eighth and Beach Ninety-seventh Streets. *Courtesy of Bob Stonehill.*

Jo-Jo the clown was perhaps the best-known advertising image for Rockaways' Playland. *Courtesy of Bill Cotter.*

The Atom Smasher roller coaster at Playland was a hit in the 1952 movie *This Is Cinerama*.

The Matterhorn was one of the more modern rides at Playland in its later years.

*Opposite, top*: Clason Point Park's ornate main entrance led visitors to a variety of amusements. *Courtesy of Fred Dahlinger Jr.*

*Opposite, middle*: Crowds in their Sunday best stroll on the midway at Clason Point Park. *Courtesy of Bob Stonehill.*

*Opposite, bottom*: Nicknamed the "inkwell," the pool provided cool relief on a hot summer's day. *Courtesy of Bob Stonehill.*

*Above*: A stern-wheeler (rear) heads off for its Great Lakes adventure. Passengers enjoyed wildlife and an Indian village before reaching the Canadian border.

*Right*: Passengers aboard the western ore buckets witnessed panoramic views of Freedomland from the southwest border to Canada.

*Opposite, top*: Circle swings and Ferris wheels were staple rides at most early amusement parks. *Courtesy of Bob Stonehill.*

*Opposite, middle*: A horse-drawn trolley pulls up at the tugboat terminal at Freedomland. The two tugboats, *Totsie* and *Pert*, each held fifty passengers.

*Opposite, bottom*: A horse provides the power for this merry-go-round at Freedomland. Note the aerial ore bucket ride to the right.

Freedomland's *Canadian* and *American* paddle-wheelers provided a pleasant and interesting cruise of the Great Lakes. Both boats were built by Todd Shipyards in Hoboken, New Jersey. They each held four hundred people.

At Freedomland, volunteer firemen wheel out the authentic replica of an 1859 pumper as they prepare to help extinguish the flames of the Great Chicago Fire of 1871.

Freedomland's Chicago Depot is now the main entrance to Clark's Trading Post amusement area in Lincoln, New Hampshire. It was brought there in the winter of 1966. *Courtesy of Clark's Trading Post.*

Klub." It was a program of goodwill provided by various amusement parks throughout the city. All that was required were three clipped coupons from different newspapers mailed to an address in Manhattan. The Kiddie Klub member received a pin in return. This pin entitled its proud owner to designated "free days" at several amusement parks throughout the city.

On Kiddie Klub Day, special performances and contests were held in addition to the free rides and attractions the youngsters enjoyed. Starlight Park held its first Kiddie Klub event on July 13, 1921. Well before opening time, workers were shocked to see several thousand children, proudly wearing their pins, ready to pour through the gates. Since many of the concessions had not yet opened for the day, the zealous youngsters made a beeline for the swimming pool, which quickly became a cacophony of squeals, laughter and splashing. By day's end, more than twenty thousand young boys and girls had entered the park's gates. The kids' particular favorites of the day were the Scrambler, the giant coaster, the Monkey Music Hall, the comedy circus and the trained elephants.

However, there was some confusion on Kiddie Day in 1922. About fifty youngsters appeared at the park just after opening time. The gateman informed the anxious gathering that Kiddie Day was being held in Luna

Starlight Park's main coaster featured a double track. Happy riders start their ascent. Also note the string of electric lights.

Park at Coney Island and not at Starlight Park that day. Apparently, there was a miscommunication. Captain Whitwell, who had become the park's manager, was summoned to the front gate. Upon engaging the smiling, energetic youngsters, he opened the gates and allowed them a "free day" at the park.

Starlight Park's actual Kiddie Klub Day that year was held on July 26, 1922. The children were mesmerized by Maharaja, the illusionist. To the kids' delight, Maharaja sawed a woman named Hazel in half. The children were astounded when she reappeared as a whole person. Zangar, the fortuneteller and mind reader, had his attendants collect written messages from the children in the audience. As soon as the messages arrived on the stage, the attendants burned the messages in full view of the curious crowd. To everyone's amazement and enjoyment, Zangar consulted his crystal ball and proceeded to recite facts about many of the children in the audience, often citing their names.

Additions in 1922 included a new sound system for the pool area. Daytime "motion pictures" were shown outside on Pearl Screens, a German innovation that did not require darkness to project its images. While the itinerary of movies changed often, there was always a short of Charlie Chaplin or Felix the Cat. In addition to rides already mentioned in previous years, Dodgem electric riding cars, the Maelstrom and the Gyroplane were up and running. Soccer matches were played and became a mainstay throughout the park's tenure.

In June 1922, the Film Players Club, with its five thousand members, held a carnival week to raise money for its benevolent fund. Each day from noon to midnight, the actors and actresses participated in baseball games and aquatic events in addition to enjoying the park's standard fare. They held special performances in the Film Players' Theater, as well as the dance pavilion. The general public was invited to attend behind-the-scenes seminars about filmmaking at various locations in the park.

As the park entered its heyday, a variety of promotional events were designed to keep the patrons coming back. A weeklong singing contest, judged by a popular soprano soloist with Bavetta's Concert Band, was held in August 1922. Baby contests, popular in many parks of the era, provided proud parents with an opportunity to showcase their babies in numerous categories, including most beautiful, best dressed and most beautiful hair, among others. Trophies and cash prizes were other incentives. A prerequisite to enter was that each child receive a free health examination by New York City Department of Health doctors. Another late season promotion was "Surprise Week," wherein a different featured act performed every day of the week. Of note was the popular vaudeville comedian Leon Morris, who performed with his pony, Madison, "the horse with a human brain."

Two events, however, put a damper on the 1922 season. In the early morning hours of May 21, just before the park was scheduled to close, an overly enthusiastic passenger aboard the roller coaster decided to stand up in his car as it rounded a curve some fifty feet above ground. The ride operator jammed on the emergency brake, but not in time. The rider died of a fractured skull, and six others were injured, three seriously. Word of the accident spread quickly as frantic relatives and friends of those who were still in the park stormed the gates in an effort to check on their loved ones.

That human tragedy was a precursor to a tragedy of another kind in November 1922. A spectacular fire completely destroyed the skating rink and dance hall located inside the Italian-inspired Exposition Hall. The hall's roof gave way under the blaze, and firemen were lucky to escape without any serious injuries. Two smaller dance halls eventually replaced the original mammoth hall. The Ferris wheel and a scenic railway were also severely damaged. Losses were assessed at $250,000.

By their nature, amusement parks of the early twentieth century were vulnerable to many devastating influences. Wood frame was the primary building material. Small fires could quickly become infernos. The parks were exposed to other elements such as electrical storms and other weather-related matters. A gale-force storm unexpectedly tore through Starlight Park on June 16, 1923. Two thousand people, mostly women, were sent into a state of panic from the crashing trees and poles. A restaurant was destroyed after it was struck by a bolt of lightning. A flagpole adjacent to the pool was severed by another strike, sending bathers fleeing for shelter until police could restore order. Ironically, many found shelter inside the spooky Old Mill. Its pitch dark tunnels only added to the night's horror.

Throughout the rest of the 1920s, episodes of accidents and crimes started to rise. A seventeen-year-old young man drowned after suffering a heart attack in July 1924. Several other drownings in the enormous pool occurred throughout the years. On August 25, 1925, eight armed gunmen robbed six employees in the check room near the pool and then went on to steal stored valuables from over two hundred bathers. The bandits exchanged gunfire with a park security official but managed to escape through a fence opening. The park official was wounded in the exchange. The young perpetrators were eventually captured.

The park's menu of activities continued to evolve through the decade, though the amusements were still the main draw. Classical music and opera

The diving platform provided many photo opportunities. Note the roller coaster in the background and the attractive bathhouses on the left. *Library of Congress.*

drew crowds. The Russian Symphony Orchestra performed *Wagner* in 1921. In 1923, the Starlight Park Stadium presented *Pagliacci* and *Il Travatore* in addition to its own Starlight Chamber Music Concerts. The 1926 season saw a fourteen-week run of classic operas before large crowds. *Rigoletto* was performed before more than five thousand people on opening night in

May of that year. *Faust, Lucia, Traviata, The Barber of Seville* and *The Masked Ball* rounded out the programs. Scores of operas would become favorites throughout the decade. When their popularity faded, sports picked up the slack. Also, for a number of years, WBNX (and also WKBQ), the Bronx's own radio station, broadcasted from the park.

Everything from horseshoe tournaments, track and field and boxing matches to soccer and baseball games kept the crowds coming. The boxing popularity at Starlight Park was tempered by the death of a boxer in the ring. In October 1926, Joseph Geraghty died as a result of blows received in a match with Bronx local Frank Leiberman. Leiberman had left the stadium unaware of the seriousness of the matter. He was arrested and detained but soon exonerated of any malicious wrongdoing.

The Eli Bridge Company's Ferris wheel underwent a transformation during its tenure at Starlight Park. It is unclear if this version predated the one seen on page 94.

Many long holdovers and some new attractions were on hand by the start of the 1927 season. The lineup included the Forest Inn. Not only did it serve as a restaurant, but also its outdoor stage was the venue for live performances and contests. The Bug House and Nonsense House were still eliciting howls of laughter. The Whip, Noah's Ark, the venerable skee-ball, the coaster, the Frolic, a Ferris wheel, the Motor Dome, the Whirlpool, the Canals of Venice and the Witching Waves were among the major attractions. Witching Waves was a flat, undulating ride where the two passenger cars traveled around an oval course. The floor was made of pliable metal that moved up and down, creating wavelike motions.

In October 1927, a startling announcement was made. The huge auditorium built for Philadelphia's Sesquicentennial Exposition in 1926 was sold to the Starlight's Amusement Company for $11,000. The original

The pool at Starlight Park was a favorite meeting point. It was one of the last operational elements of the park. *Bronx County Historical Society.*

$500,000 structure was dismantled, and its steel ribs would be reconstructed on 177th Street and DeVoe Avenue adjacent to the park's amusement border. It took fifty-five railroad cars to deliver the pieces. It was advertised as "the largest auditorium in the world." Sporting events and some other major entertainment attractions would be moved from the park's open-air facility to the covered auditorium (operas continued to operate out of the open-air facility). It was initially named the Bronx Coliseum but was later renamed the New York Coliseum (not to be confused with Manhattan's coliseum of the same name). In some advertisements, it was referred to as Starlight Park Stadium. The 105,000-square-foot venue had an original seating capacity of around fifteen thousand, although Starlight's management later claimed that it would double that after alterations. It is doubtful that any of those improvements ever came to fruition.

Starting in 1929, the coliseum (or stadium) hosted musical events, auto racing, circuses, professional boxing and wrestling matches and a plethora of other events. It was also the home of the New York Giants soccer team. In the spring of that year, the Ringling Brothers Barnum & Bailey Circus kicked off its season with a ten-day run at the facility. Some of its featured acts were Ugo "the Human Projectile," a herd of twenty-eight elephants, aerialist Lillian Leitzel and world-famous high-wire performer Willie Wallenda. The circus returned in 1930 for another ten-day engagement. Attendance was off from the previous year, and visitors at one show were horrified when a performer on the pole-balancing act fell forty feet to his death. That year also saw an overhaul of the swimming pool and additions to the bathhouses. The "Five Cents Nights" promotion proved popular. A customer paid five cents each for all the rides and attractions in the park after a designated hour. But boxing was becoming the big draw. Fights were booked whenever Madison Square Garden had no matches scheduled. The first boxing event at the new venue was on April 12, 1929.

Trying to keep up with the competition as the Great Depression loomed, park management brought in a few more modern rides, including the Snap o' the Whip, Noah's Ark, an upgraded scooter ride and the Tilt-a-Whirl. Rides were either fifteen or twenty cents, somewhat less than at Luna Park at Coney Island and Palisades Amusement Park. Frequent promotions were held to keep the crowds coming. Contests, ladies' nights, free admission days and swimming competitions were among them. But by this time, the glory years were quickly coming to an end. The rides were poorly maintained and were becoming outdated. More "flesh" acts were added since they were more cost efficient than adding new rides. Tawdry side shows came along.

At the park's peak around 1926, business records indicate there were twenty-six rides and 150 concessions. By 1935, the numbers had diminished to fourteen rides and a paltry 20 concessions. A miniature golf course was constructed on the site of the old Witching Waves attraction in 1931. A new roller rink came along that year as well.

The end of the Starlight Park amusement era was a protracted affair with no definitive closing date. But perhaps a major blow occurred on August 6, 1932. Fifteen thousand people witnessed a large fire consume part of Starlight Park. The abandoned roller coaster and several other concessions, including the Canals of Venice and a shooting gallery, were badly damaged.

Nonetheless, the park soldiered on through the Great Depression years. The swimming pool generated revenue while continuing to filter three million gallons of salt water daily. The coliseum, the athletic fields and the picnic areas became the focal points, but the revenue generated was not sufficient to support the park as a whole. In addition to the other events, political rallies helped keep the coliseum solvent. The Communist Party held several rallies at the venue. Its rally in May 1935 was attended by over six thousand supporters.

The grounds were spruced up in 1933 as park manager Captain Whitwell threw his efforts behind creating a recreational center. The rides were no longer in his plans. A beach club, handball courts, tennis courts, sun lamps and exercise machines were introduced to stave off a total closing. However, the adjacent coliseum was still going strong. Popular lightweight champion Barney Ross battled Billy Petrolle before a large crowd in 1934. The event spurred the venue once again into direct competition with Madison Square Garden. Around this time, Bill Harkin replaced Captain Whitwell as park manager.

But by 1940, the park was operating under the receivership of James R. Murphy. Part of the New York Coliseum and Starlight Park were sold at auction. The properties were described as containing a swimming pool and a venue for "midget" auto races, boxing, wrestling and other sports events. Richard F. Mount, the new owner, indicated that operations would continue temporarily, pending other legal matters.

In May 1941, Mount leased the acreage with its extant structures to a syndicate headed by Robert Kaplan. A series of subleases indicated that the park would be invigorated beginning with improvements in the pool and the bathhouses. Additions of more handball courts, tennis courts and plans for night baseball games, basketball games and college track meets led Mr. Kaplan to claim that the park would be like a small edition of the World's Fair. It is unknown exactly how many of these improvements ever got off the ground. Clearly, the rides and carnival atmosphere were gone. Around 1942, Tex O'Rourke was managing the park. But with World War II in full gear, the U.S. Army took over the coliseum and used it as a vehicle maintenance center from 1942 to 1946.

On July 17, 1946, another fire destroyed the two-story bathhouses, marking the end of an era. The property was condemned. Plans were made for the removal of the pool to allow access for the construction of the Cross Bronx Expressway under the direction of Robert Moses. Soccer teams continued to use a portion of the grounds into the 1950s.

Today, another park, not far from the original, maintains the name Starlight Park. It includes baseball fields, soccer fields, spray showers and playgrounds. It is located along the Sheridan Expressway between East 174$^{th}$ Street and East 172$^{nd}$ Street. Civic groups have been working with New York City park officials to make it a safe and pleasant park for young and old alike.

## Clason Point

Clason Point is a peninsula on the southeastern shore of the Bronx jutting out into the East River and Long Island Sound. Over the years, the name has changed from Cornell's Neck to Clason Point. The point got its name from Isaac Clason, a Scottish merchant and major landowner on the point about 1793.

One of the first European settlers to build a home on Clason Point was Thomas Cornell in 1643. The house was expanded several times over the years. Clinton Stephens bought the property when he retired from business around 1899. Stephens was an engineer who had been contracted to enlarge the Erie Canal. He also built the Erie Railroad, the Albany and Susquehanna Railroad and several railroad tunnels.

Clinton turned the house into an inn and made it the focus of Clason Point Park. The dinners served there were equal in quality to the food available in the finest Manhattan restaurants. Patrons of the inn had a choice of eating in the elegant dining room or on the broad piazza with its view of the sound. The walls of the dining room were covered with Dutch panel paintings and English hunting posters. The history of the house was inscribed on a side wall printed in old-fashioned lettering. Over the years, the name of the inn changed from Clason Point Inn to Gilligan's Inn and, finally, to simply the Historic Inn.

In addition to the inn, the point had a merry-go-round, a soda fountain and a candy stand. In 1907, a German woman who ran the last two concessions was, by all accounts, an attraction all by herself. She would amuse her customers so much that they always left with smiles. A bathing pavilion and a sand beach lined the shore, where visitors could catch a few rays of sun or swim in Long Island Sound.

Stephens was a smart businessman. He owned and operated his own ferry service to bring visitors to the point. The ferry ran from 138th Street in Manhattan to Clason Point. Initially, people came to the point by ferry, either from Manhattan or College Point, or by motorboat. Upon arrival, one would find the bathing pavilion to the right of the pier. On the left was the casino, where patrons could dance away the day or night. Farther to the left was the inn.

Billie Burke's *Wild West* show was a highlight at Clason Point in 1909. Burke's show featured real cowboys, Indians, cowgirls, bronco busters, sharpshooters and lariat experts. A genuine cowboy band played for the performances.

In 1910, when trolley service was expanded to the point, it brought more people from the Bronx and Westchester to the park. The fact that it could be reached by a fare of only five cents from anywhere in the Bronx with free admission became a major drawing feature of the park. Members of government and the social elite attended the opening of Clason Point Park

Trolleys often delivered visitors to the main entrance of Clason Point Park. *Courtesy of Bob Stonehill.*

in 1910. The park was decorated with flags of all nations for the occasion. A fifty-piece military band was brought in to entertain the crowds all day and all night long. The evening culminated in a spectacular display of fireworks.

Initially, the rides included a new circle swing, a mile-long Forest Coaster, Shooting the Chutes, the Double Whirl, Peary at the North Pole and the Lemon Show. Blake's Animal Circus was another new attraction at the park. In addition, there was Berger's shooting gallery and roughly one hundred other concessions.

Around this time, the inn was under the management of Edward Gilligan. Joseph Cowan's Palace Casino was remodeled with an addition that extended 280 feet over the water.

There was a new saltwater swimming pool fed by water from Long Island Sound that was not filtered. The pool measured three hundred feet long by fifty feet wide. Over time, the water in the pool became so dark that locals called it "the inkwell."

The point changed dramatically in 1910 with the opening of Fairyland Park, a full-service amusement park. It covered twenty acres and included its own bathing beach. Five acres were set aside to create a lagoon, walking paths and miniature waterfalls. The rest of the property was dedicated to outdoor and indoor entertainment.

One of the most popular rides at Fairyland was a carousel owned by Frederick Dolle. Dolle leased a brand-new, seventy-five- by seventy-five-foot carousel house on Clason Point Road. According to his business partner, M.D. Borrelli, Dolle's company, F. Dolle's Carrousel Works (later Dolle's Carousel Works and Dolle's Carrousels), would build three or four carousels a year during the off season. Borrelli claimed they manufactured everything needed to create carousels except for the horses. These were usually carved by Charles Carmel. The company was noted for embedding reflective jewels on its carousel figures and chariots.

Across the road from the park, the Clason Point Aquarama Company built a new water ride. Adjoining it, the Clason Point Amusement Company erected a twin racing coaster. The Clason Point Twin Coaster Company, which was incorporated by Albert Turpin, Edgar Turpin and Arthur F. Turpin, claimed that the point was "the new Coney Island of New York City." It advertised that it was looking to expand operations at the park by adding a variety of new attractions, whether big or small.

In September 1910, a baby contest was held at Ed Gilligan's Historic Inn. It featured five thousand youngsters. The original judges were so overwhelmed by the prospect of judging so many contestants that they decided to opt out of the event. Five new judges were selected, and they spent the better part of five hours deliberating to determine the winners. The first place winner, Edward J. Cullen, twenty-two months old, won a go-cart. The original first place prize was to go to Edna Gilligan, two years old, but her father owned the inn. In a kind gesture, he allowed his daughter to accept only an honorary mention.

A storm that raged through New York City on June 11 and 12, 1911, caused over $1 million in damage and did not spare Clason Point Park. The Ferris wheel, carrying several passengers, was blown off its axis and rendered immobile. When lightning struck the wheel, it temporarily blinded the passengers, and panic ensued. Several women tried to jump from the wheel but were restrained by the other passengers. Rescuers were able to extricate them with the assistance of several ladders rigged together. Another storm that same summer routed four hundred tent campers from Higgs Beach, a summer campground on Clason Point from around 1898 until 1924. The storm lasted twelve hours, and when it was over, the camp was completely ruined by a combination of high winds and heavy rain.

The *Bronx Home News* sponsored a free children's day at Clason Point Park in 1911. It was reported that over ten thousand children attended the park that day.

The rides at the point included a roller coaster operated by H. Emmert Butterfield, the Frolic, a Ferris wheel, a circle swing, Witching Waves, a big bamboo slide and a carousel run by Eugene McGuire of the Fairmont Amusement Company. A circus was performed each day. In addition, there was a pony and goat cart track. Ben Dubinsky ran a successful penny arcade. A roller-skating rink operated by Mr. Cooper and a refurbished Red Mill run by Neville Bayley were located outside the park.

One of the carousels at Clason Point was the Philadelphia Toboggan Company's PTC #14, code named the "Qualtri." This carousel was manufactured in 1906 and was originally at Melville Park in Bayonne, New Jersey. It was moved to Clason Point and then became Tirelli's carousel at South Beach in Staten Island. In 1920, the carousel was sent to Rocky Point in Moosic, Pennsylvania, which later changed its name to Ghost Town in the Glen.

Clason Point drew large crowds in fair weather. The location made it ideal for families from the Bronx, Manhattan and nearby Westchester County. The Stephenses, both father and son, ran the park with the goal of keeping it friendly and safe for all visitors. No rowdy behavior was tolerated in the park. Clason Point Park had its own police force

# Lost Amusement Parks of New York City

The boardwalk inside Clason Point Park was often very crowded. The owner, Clinton Stephens, advertised in 1911 that the previous season's attendance was 1.5 million. *Courtesy of Bob Stonehill.*

to ensure that it remained peaceful and family friendly. When Clinton Stephens, owner of the park for over thirteen years, died in 1915, his son Clinton Stephens Jr. continued to run the park. By 1916, the inn could accommodate more than one thousand people. On a good day, attendance at the park could reach fifty thousand.

M.J. Kane's was a major saloon in the 1920s adjoining Clason Point Park. Kane's daughter Helen often sang at the saloon. It was Helen who coined the phrase "Boop-oop-a-doop." Betty Boop, the cartoon flapper, was modeled after her.

On June 12, 1922, a terrible tragedy occurred when the one-hundred-foot Ferris wheel at Clason Point was blown over in a wind storm. On the day of the accident, thousands of people had come to the park to escape the high humidity. The visitors had virtually no warning before the storm struck. The sky suddenly turned black, but there was nary a breath of wind before the gale started. The weather bureau stated that the gusts reached up to one hundred miles per hour. In addition to the wind, torrential rain and numerous lightning strikes added to the danger of the storm.

At the time of the accident, approximately eighty passengers were on board the giant Ferris wheel. Witnesses reported that the wheel seemed to be lifted up and thrown into Long Island Sound. Moments later, the lower part of the wheel collapsed onto the beach (ten feet below), burying riders under the wreckage. It took volunteers, policemen and firemen over a half hour to remove the victims, some of whom were unconscious. The victims were taken to a nearby recreation pier to await the arrival of doctors and ambulances.

A houseboat docked at the pier was damaged when a support beam from the Ferris wheel crashed down and split the cabin apart. Mrs. Marie Tolberg, whose father ran a motorboat between Whitestone and Clason Point, was found unconscious. Her body was shielding her one-year-old baby. She had rushed into the cabin after the crash to protect her child. Neither she nor the baby was seriously injured.

At the scene, the death toll was recorded at seven. That total increased as some of the initial thirty-five injured eventually succumbed. The storm was reported to have been one of the worst ever to strike New York City. The damage city-wide was estimated at $1.5 million. Building inspectors were ordered to inspect every ride in the city as a result of the storm. Paul Simon, the owner of the wheel, was brought to court and charged with homicide for failing to evacuate the ride when he observed the approaching storm. A grand jury was called to investigate the accident. In August, the charge of homicide was dropped when an engineer testified that the Ferris wheel had been well constructed. In addition, a weatherman testified that the storm was the most severe since 1871.

The park quickly resumed operations. Some of the acts performing in that same year at the Ferry Casino were the Trinity Trio (Frank Wallace, Lou Wallace and Eddie Hart), Jack Egan, Frank Lippy, Joe Melnery, Push-Push the Wop and George K. Hackett, the dancing clown. On Wednesday nights, Basiloue's Society Entertainers and the Twirling Amateurs were the featured performers.

Just four months after the Ferris wheel tragedy, a fire caused $10,000 worth of damage to the amusement area at Clason Point Park. The fire started behind the Old Mill. People cheered as the building burned because the electric piano that played one tune over and over was finally silenced. Realizing the Old Mill was beyond saving, firemen turned their attention to the Red Racer and an adjacent carousel, which were being showered with sparks.

The former Fairyland Dance Hall, a two-story wooden structure in Clason Point Park, burned to the ground on July 29, 1931. The building was no longer a dance hall but was being used as a studio by Hugo Gerber. By the time the firemen arrived, the building was too far gone to be saved. The estimated value of the damage was $100,000.

Fairyland opened in 1910 at Clason Point. It quickly became a popular amusement destination along with Clason Point Park. *Courtesy of Bob Stonehill.*

The demise of Clason Point Park was brought about by a combination of things. First was the Great Depression. People no longer had extra money to spend on amusements. Second, the Long Island Sound was becoming more and more polluted, causing officials to discourage swimming in the waters off the point. Last, the automobile played a major part in the decline of the amusement park. People now were free to travel wherever they wished and were no longer restricted to using public transportation.

Mal Deitch and Dr. Joseph Goodstein bought the property in 1947. They created the Shorehaven Beach Club on the property of the old Clason Point Amusement Park in 1949. The club featured a modern swimming pool, a kiddie pool and open-air entertainment that included dancing to popular big bands of the time.

Shortly after the Shorehaven Beach Club closed in 1986, the property became a combination of condominiums, public housing and private homes.

## Freedomland

"Mommy, daddy, take my hand. Take me out to Freedomland."

The above jingle was heard by millions throughout the New York City metropolitan area during the early 1960s. The advertisement was designed to entice families to visit what was dubbed the "Disneyland of the East."

This book focuses on the rise and fall of amusement parks in New York City in the first half of the twentieth century. But Freedomland's history was so fleeting and extraordinary that it merits an exception. The following pages will not be an in-depth look into this park, as it has been chronicled quite thoroughly elsewhere. Details on its variety of attractions can be tracked down quite easily.

By the 1950s, automobiles had become the primary mode of transportation in the country. Families were now able to travel to more distant and remote locations for entertainment. The advent of theme parks provided a good match. New York State had its Storytown, U.S.A. at Lake George (1949) and Frontier Town in North Hudson (1952). But these parks paled in comparison when Disneyland opened its gates on July 17, 1955. One of Walt Disney's chief designers and planners of the project was Cornelius Vanderbilt (C.V.) Wood Jr., who soon became Disneyland's first vice-president.

Wood, born in Oklahoma and raised in Texas, had an intense work ethic. When Wood was asked about his fascination with theme parks, he replied,

"I view it as imaginative combination of big business, show business, design creativity and mass education through entertainment. What more could a person want?" As early as 1957, Wood envisioned a theme park to dramatize the American heritage. He teamed with, among others, M.T. Ted Raynor, president of the International Recreation Corporation, which later became the parent company of Freedomland. In a similar vein to Wood's philosophy, Raynor stated, "Bringing history to life by re-creating it is an enchanting way to engage both young and old."

The project was announced by William Zeckendorf Sr. in May 1959. Zeckendorf's company, Webb and Knapp, owned 400 acres of marshland in the Baychester section of the northeast Bronx. Webb and Knapp leased 205 acres to the International Recreation Corporation. Approximately 85 acres would be devoted to its themed areas. The location seemed ideal. It was accessible by bus, train and automobile. At the time, the New York metropolitan area's population was over fifteen million. Projections of annual patronage soared as high as five million. On May 26, 1959, the *News York Times* reported that Freedomland's costs were soaring well above estimates and eventually ballooned to $65 million. That figure far surpassed the amount invested in Disneyland.

Groundbreaking ceremonies took place on August 26, 1960. A "country" was built in about three hundred days by well over two thousand people as Freedomland's themed area took shape, roughly emulating an outline of the United States. Aberthaw Construction and Turner Construction provided most of the manpower and machinery to get the job done.

Seven major themed areas were scattered throughout the park representing life, for the most part, in the nineteenth century: Little Old New York, Old Chicago, New Orleans, Satellite City (an exception), the Great Plains, the Old Southwest and San Francisco. Within each area, numerous attractions were designed to inform and entertain.

The park opened on Father's Day, June 19, 1960. Over sixty thousand guests poured into the park. Parking lots and surrounding roads were jammed. Satellite City and some smaller concessions were not ready for the crowd's exploration. Frederick Schumacher, Freedomland's general manager, boldly predicted that Freedomland would become a popular New York City destination on par with Central Park and the Statue of Liberty.

Freedomland started with forty-one attractions (Disneyland began with twenty-two in 1955). The attractions were too numerous to detail here. Suffice it to say that "crossing the country" provided one thrill and adventure after another. On a busy day, one could walk around Macy's original store (with attendants in period dress), check out the F. and M. Schaefer Brewing Company, take a tugboat ride in the harbor and ride a horse-drawn trolley, among other attractions just in Little Old New York alone.

Children loved "putting out" the Great Chicago Fire. There were shootouts in the Great Plains. San Francisco featured an indoor ride of the great 1906 earthquake in addition to Chinatown and seals in the bay area. There were boat rides in the Pacific Northwest. Burro rides, a ride through mine caverns, an opera house and a saloon entertained guests in the Old Southwest. In New Orleans, one could celebrate Mardi Gras, take a wagon ride through a Civil War battlefield and enjoy a meal at the Plantation Restaurant. Two great paddle-wheelers plied the Great Lakes.

One could step into the future at Satellite City, ride narrow-gauge railroads, "drive" antique cars, ride an aerial ore bucket across the country, watch fireworks and enjoy concerts at the Moon Bowl, featuring the greatest stars and bands of the day. Attention to detail was critical, including the five thousand original costumes designed by Gordon Weiss.

But dark clouds quickly appeared on the horizon. First-year guests totaled just under two million, well below projections. Freedomland was in debt. Liens were filed, including one by Turner Construction for $3,600,000. Lawsuits were filed by patrons injured in the park.

The 1961 season saw the institution of a "pay one price" admission policy ($2.95) and the addition of more standard amusement rides, a trend that would continue until the park closed. Other new attractions at the newly built Hollywood Arena included gladiators in combat, jousting knights, chariot races and the "Charge of the Bengal Lancers" as the park started to stray from its initial focus on American heritage. Despite these modifications, attendance figures failed to impress.

Along with the trend to becoming more of an amusement park, $1 million was invested in new rides in 1962. The Astro-Ride coaster from the Allan Herschell Company was added. This was accompanied by the Wiggly Worm, a caterpillar ride. In 1963, the Meteor, a "used" single-rail coaster, was brought to the park. Bumper cars, side shows and a Last Supper wax display were in evidence. A rebuilt Dentzel carousel, with its four rows of horses, chariots and menagerie animals, graced the grounds. The American history theme was gradually becoming more of an afterthought.

On April 22, 1964, the New York's World Fair opened, adding to Freedomland's woes by siphoning off even more customers. In 1964, the World's Fair drew around twenty-seven million people. Freedomland's admissions revenue dropped below $1 million. By the end of the season, on

September 14, 1964, Freedomland was in bankruptcy. The park's run was over after only five seasons, a remarkably short run for any entertainment park, especially one of its magnitude.

There has been much conjecture about the reasons for Freedomland's demise. The emergence of the World's Fair is often cited as the primary culprit, but the park's finances were in disarray well before then. Initial cost overruns and union work rules contributed. The park was subject to New York's fickle weather, unlike the twelve-month sunny season in California's Disneyland. The costs of winterizing the park came at a greater price than anticipated. The waterways (including the Great Lakes) had to be drained after each season into the Hutchinson River, only to be refilled in the spring.

The landfill areas provided weak support for many buildings and attractions, resulting in unexpected repair costs. Some even speculate that the landowners were looking forward to the park's closure and were just waiting for the land to be zoned for housing in order to turn a profit.

The concept of Freedomland itself may have been a contributory cause. Freedomland's identity confused some. Some historians felt it somehow diminished the past (which included some factual inaccuracies). On the other hand, amusement buffs, at least those not very interested in history, traveled to Palisades Amusement Park, Rye Playland or Coney Island for bigger thrill rides.

By the spring of 1966, almost all traces of Freedomland were gone. In May 1966, work began on the construction of the mammoth Co-op City housing complex, where over fifty thousand people now reside. With the addition of the Bay Plaza Shopping Center, Freedomland's area was blanketed with the two projects.

Not everything was lost in the transition from theme park to housing project. Charles Wood, owner of both Gaslight Village and Storytown, U.S.A. (now Six Flags Great Escape) in Lake George, New York, purchased the Dentzel carousel. Wood also acquired the popular Danny the Dragon ride and the Crystal Maze (also known as the House of Mirrors) for the opening of its 1966 season. Shortly thereafter, he purchased the Mine Caverns and the Tornado Adventure (1967). The Tornado, a dark adventure ride, had a brief stint in Kennywood Park in Pennsylvania before its debut at Lake George. It is believed to be in storage now. Danny the Dragon did not transfer well, as its underground magnetic wire system often failed, eventually leading to its demise. Only a handful of Danny the Dragon rides were built, and one still operates in San Jose, California.

Some buildings made their way to Magic Mountain in Boulder, Colorado. The Pirate Gun Gallery found a new home in Niagara Falls. It is believed that none of the above Freedomland attractions operates today.

However, one can still enjoy a sense of what Freedomland once was. The *Canadian*, one of the two Great Lakes paddle-wheelers, is currently the home of Dot and Bill's Showboat Restaurant in Port Chester, New York. Clark's Trading Post in Lincoln, New Hampshire, purchased the Santa Fe Railroad Depot and the San Francisco Railroad Depot during the winter of 1966. Some of Little Old New York's bricks are in evidence in the park, as are numerous street lamps.

It is likely that no other entertainment park, particularly one of its magnitude, could match Freedomland's dramatic rise and meteoric fall. Though a financial failure, it entertained millions. Its planners and builders, who built a "country" in three hundred days, displayed the can-do entrepreneurial spirit often represented in the park's patriotic theme.

# INDEX

**A**

Abrams, Sam 82, 83
Artistic Carousell Company 65

**B**

Bakken 9
Beachland Amusements 43
Beachy, Lincoln 38
Belt Parkway 68
Borrelli, M.D. 108
Bowery Bay Beach Improvement
 Company 71, 73, 83
Boyton, Paul 11
Bronx International Exposition 91

**C**

Canarsie Amusement Company 56, 61
Carmel, Charles 108
carousels
 Bostock's "Rounders" 22
 Dentzel 115, 116
 Dolle 108
 Harton 59
 Junction Carousel 73
 Looff 36, 47, 72, 73, 77
 Maple Carrousel 75
 Murphy's 40, 64, 65, 68
 Nunley's 7, 40, 68, 69
 PTC #14 40, 109
 PTC #15 29, 31
 Silver Spring 72
Clark's Trading Post 117
Clason Point Amusement Company 108
Coney Island 11, 14, 17, 20, 22, 23,
 27, 30, 41, 47, 54, 57, 60, 65,
 75, 77, 98, 104, 108, 116
Co-op City 116

**D**

Daufkirch, Henry 73
Disneyland 12, 113, 114, 116
Dodgem Company 41, 66, 98
Dolle, Frederick 108
Dreamland 11, 20, 60, 77
Droge, Fred 77, 80
Dundy, Elmer "Skip" 11, 20, 22, 57

# INDEX

## E

Ehret, George  71, 73, 74, 83
Eli Bridge Company  93

## F

Fairyland Park  108, 111
Ferris, George  10
Fort George Amusement Company  19, 28, 30
Fort Wendel  25, 26
Frontier Town  113

## G

Gala Park  74, 75, 77, 79, 80, 81, 82, 83, 84
Gaslight City  116
Geist, A. Joseph  86, 89
Geist, Richard  89
Gilligan, Edward  108
Gish, Lillian  25
Goldberg, Edward  83
Golden City Arena  66, 67
Golden City Theater  57, 60
Goldstein, Harry  64
Graham, James S.  51, 52
Great Depression  11, 91, 104, 105, 113
Griffiths, James A.  36, 40

## H

Happyland  36, 37, 38, 39, 40, 41
Hergenhan, Albert  36, 40
Hinchliffe, John  46, 48
Hinchliffe, William  51
Hippodrome  20, 38, 57
Hirsch, Benjamin  83

## I

International Recreation Corporation  114

## J

Jones's Wood  10, 18
Joytown  88

## K

Kane, M.J.  110
Keenan, Vernon  89
Kiralfy, Bolosy  36
Kremer, George W.  72, 73, 80, 84

## L

Levitt, Victor D.  38
Loew, Marcus  19, 30
Luna Park  11, 20, 22, 59, 60, 77, 98, 104

## M

Mangels, William  23, 64, 77
McGarvie, Harry F.  92, 93, 95, 96
Midland Beach Company  46
Morris Amusement Company  75
Morris, E. Joy  27, 28, 29, 75, 81, 83, 84, 99
Moses, Robert  68, 106
Mount, Richard F.  105
movies
  *Sophie's Choice*  88
  *This Is Cinerama*  90
Munger, L.A.  76, 79, 80
Murphy, Timothy  65

## N

New York Coliseum  104, 105
New York's World Fair  89, 115
North Beach Amusement Company  83
Nunley, William  65

## O

Old Barrel  19
O'Rourke, Tex  106

## P

Palisades Amusement Park  17, 28, 65, 67, 104, 116
Paradise Park  19, 20, 22, 24, 26, 28, 29, 30

# Index

Philadelphia Toboggan Company 22, 40, 109
Prohibition 11, 73, 82

## Q

Queen's Park 83

## R

Raynor, Ted 114
Ringling Brothers Barnum and Bailey Circus 60, 104
Roller Coasters
  Atom Smasher 89
  Blue Streak 10
  Clason Point Twin Coaster 108
  Coliseum 59
  Cyclone 65
  Dips 40
  Gravity Wonder 86
  Joy Ride Through Clouds 93
  Roller Boller Coaster 40
  Rough Rider 22, 23
  Thompson's Scenic Railroad 30, 36, 46, 48, 85
  Whirlwind Racer 48
Roosevelt, Franklin D. 41, 52
Rosenthal, Irving 30, 65, 66, 67
Rosenthal, Jacob 30, 65, 66, 67
Rye Playland 116

## S

Schenck Brothers Palisade Park 23, 30
Schenck, Joseph 18, 19, 27, 29, 30
Schenck, Nicholas 18, 19, 28, 30
Schultheis, John F. 18
Schumacher, Frederick 114
Seltz, William 76, 81
Shad Link 78
Sheen, Milton 67
Shorehaven Beach Club 113
South Beach Amusement Company 36
South Beach Amusement Park 42, 43
Spring Lake 72
Starlight Park Stadium 100, 104

Steeplechase Park, Coney Island 11
Steeplechase Park, Rockaway 85
Stein, Solomon 64
Steinway, William 71, 73
Stella Park 76, 77, 78, 79, 80, 81, 83
Stephens, Clinton 110
Stephens, Clinton, Jr. 110
Storytown, U.S.A. 113, 116
Streep, Meryl 90

## T

Thomas, Lowell 88
Thompson, Frederic 11, 20, 22, 27, 57
Thompson, L.A. 36, 46, 48, 85, 86, 93
Thompson's Park 85, 86
Tickler 23
Tilyou, George C. 11, 85
Tirelli, Henry 40, 41, 109
Traver Circle Swing Company 48, 54, 56, 61, 74

## V

Vanderbilt, Cornelius 113
Vauxhall Gardens 9

## W

Warner, William J., Jr. 54, 56, 57, 61, 62, 63, 64, 65
Wendel, Captain Louis 26
Whitwell, Captain 98, 105
Wood, Charles 116
Woodcliff Pleasure Park 10
Woodland Beach 44, 45, 46, 51
Works Progress Administration 41, 52, 85
World Columbian Exposition 10

## Z

Zeckendorf, William, Sr. 114

# ABOUT THE AUTHORS

Wesley and Barbara Gottlock are retired educators who have a passion for the history of New York City and the Hudson Valley. This is their fifth book and the first devoted to a bygone era of New York City. Wes and Barbara are popular speakers, and they have presented well over one hundred lectures pertaining to local history. In addition, they are docents and volunteer coordinators for tours to Bannerman Island in the Hudson River. They reside in New Windsor, New York, overlooking the majestic Hudson. Visit their website at www.gottlockbooks.com.

*Visit us at*
www.historypress.net

*This title is also available as an e-book*